Bible Study: Defending Daniel

The Book of Daniel
Except it or Accept it

Rickard B DeMille

MacDonald, Barclay & Co. ◇ Little Elm, Texas

A MacDonald, Barclay & Co. book

MacDonald, Barclay & Co. (www.macdonaldbarclay.com) is a very new, very small press located in the also very small town of Little Elm, Texas. MacDonald, Barclay specializes in whatever demands our attention. We have a small but talented group of authors covering a broad genre range.

ALL RIGHTS RESERVED. No part of this work covered by the copyright herein may be reproduced or used in any form or by an means—graphic, electronic, or mechanical, including photocopying, recording, taping, Web distribution, or information storage and retrieval systems—without the prior written permission of MacDonald, Barclay & Co.

For more information, or permission to use material from this text, contact us by:
Email: info@macdonaldbarclay.com
Mail: MacDonald, Barclay & Co.
Suite 100-436
2701 Little Elm Parkway
Little Elm, TX 75068

Copyright © 2012 by Rickard B DeMille

ISBN: **0615635741**
ISBN-13: **978-0615635743**

DEDICATION

This book is dedicated to everyone who holds the Bible dear, and believes that God is active in the lives of his children. I pray that everyone who reads this work will gain a deeper and stronger love for the Truth and faith in the Word.

CONTENTS

Preface 1

Chapter 1 5
Introduction 5
Statement of the Problem 8
Definition of Terms 9
Limitations of the Study 9
Final Comments 10

Chapter 2 11
Outline of the Book of Daniel 11
Historical Summary 20

Chapter 3 23
Section 1: Introduction 23
Section 2: Unity of the Book 25
Section 3: Direct Historical Arguments 29
Section 4: General Historical Arguments 98
Section 5: Linguistic Arguments 117
Section 6: Conclusion 142
Section 7: Final Observations 148

Chapter 4 155
Section 1: Review 155
Section 2: Discussion 156
Section 3: Interpretation 160

Appendix: 163
Expanded Historical Outline 163

Glossary 181

Bibliography 187

Endnotes 191

ACKNOWLEDGMENTS

I would like to offer a deep and sincere thanks to all
of the faculty and staff of
Golden State School of Theology,
for their hard work and commitment to spreading the
Gospel of Christ throughout the world. They have my
admiration and respect for the thousands of hours of
labor, learning and prayer they offer from their love of
Christ. May God Bless them and their work.

PREFACE

I wrote this text eleven years ago as a master's thesis, originally titled *Daniel: An Analysis*. It was written as part of the requirements for my Masters of Ministry in Biblical Studies from Golden State School of Theology, and answered one of the most perplexing questions arising from my outside study of the Old Testament.

Why do scholars and academics claim that Daniel is not what Christians believe it to be – a book of prophecy? This book is meant to answer that question.

I considered rewriting it completely, making it more conversational and less formal, but that would have made it longer as well. I opted for brevity. Some may find this book dry, but hope they also find it educational, well researched, and to the point.

This effort, *The Book of Daniel: Except It Or Accept It*, represents almost a year and a half of constant commitment, research, composition and prayer. It represents more than a thousand of hours spent at my desk with my Bible and reference books, or at the Southern Methodist University religion library some distance away. Instead of sleeping, taking in a movie, or sitting on the couch watching TV with my family, I labored to expand my understanding of Scripture.

Golden State School of Theology, GSST, was chosen for several reasons. The curriculum is excellent. This is not a "diploma mill," but a true educational program. It required a significant amount of work, on my part and on the part of the exceptional faculty there. For these reasons, GSST was unquestionably the best educational value.

Golden State School of Theology was wonderful. My deepest and most sincere thanks go out to everyone there for their teachings, love, and support. They even allowed me to continue participating in the school after my grauation on October 6, 2001. I assisted, where possible, with the preparation of course material. This proved to be a unique and humbling experience. Even more humbling was the honor of receiving a Masters of Divinity a year later.

As mentioned above, the last requirement in the Masters of Ministry program was the preparation of a thesis. Very early in my studies, I felt a special interest in the ancient Middle East. I have always loved history, and this period seemed to draw me in. Midway through the coursework I completed a study of the book of Daniel. I was surprised to learn that almost all Biblical scholars believed the book of Daniel was not historical, or factual. Most considered it "pscudcpigraphal," meaning it was written by someone other than the stated author – a man who simply claimed to be Daniel the prophet. It was written in Daniel's name to give it more authority than it deserved.

I subsequently read commentaries and summaries by the most respected experts. I analyzed and pondered their arguments and assertions and found them compelling, well reasoned, and impossible to refute.

Somewhat confused, I continued my classes, completed the coursework, and began to consider what topic I should propose for the thesis. As I reviewed my classes, I immediately recognized that I wanted to learn even more about the ancient Middle East. I remembered my fascination with the one hundred year period starting at about 630 B.C. when the Assyrians were conquered by the Chaldeans/Babylonians, and the Medes were overthrown by the Cyrus and the Persians, who went on to defeat the Babylonians as well.

The Chaldean Kings of Babylon were in power for less than a century, but their significance in the history of Israel was immense. The Jewish nation was destroyed, carried off into captivity in Babylon (the 1st Diaspora). They lost the center of their religious life when Solomon's Temple was destroyed, and were forced to develop a system of worship and study that would eventually result in the establishment of synagogues. This religious adaptation would allow the Jewish people to maintain their cultural and spiritual identity, through centuries of exile and persecution, until today.

Furthermore, as you have certainly realized by now, this is the period in which the Book of Daniel was written - or set, depending on your point of view. As I researched deeper into this period, looking for a specific subject on which to concentrate my efforts, small contradictions to the prevailing skepticism regarding the authenticity of Daniel began to appear. These small contradictions then grew into nagging questions.

Before long, I had a subject for my thesis. Simply stated, I wanted to know the reasons why almost all experts agreed that Daniel was written centuries after its stated date. I wanted to determine whether these reasons were valid. Finally, if they were valid, was there an alternative explanation that still allowed for the authenticity of the Book of Daniel.

What I found was fascinating, faith promoting, and rewarding. As I clicked "Save" on the final version of my thesis, I did so with not only a greater understanding, but a deeper faith in the inspired origin of Daniel. Those conclusions, in turn, inspired the title of this book.

The Book of Daniel: Except It Or Accept It, is the challenge I issue to everyone who reads my analysis of Daniel. There are specific standards which apply to the study of ancient texts, especially canonical texts. I encountered several topics where dating methods and other standards of evaluation for the Bible in general, and Book of Daniel in particular, were given with a footnote: "except for the Book of Daniel." I will go into greater detail about these exclusions, but the bottom line is this: stating the rules for evaluation apply "except for the Book of Daniel," then failing to give it an impartial examination of what the exception means, is not acceptable. If you are forced to "except" basic facts regarding the analysis of this scripture, which are universally applied to other ancient texts, then maybe you need to reconsider those facts. In my opinion, you are really left with no choice but to "accept" *Daniel* for what it claims to be, the most revelatory book in the Old Testament.

CHAPTER 1

Introduction

The Book of Daniel is one of the most important books in the Old Testament; it's certainly one of the most prophetic and therefore controversial. The wonderfully inspired nature of this book offers Christian and Jewish scholars, as well as all believers in ancient scripture, a source of faith, inspiration, and detailed study that has endured for centuries. An understanding of Daniel is almost essential for understanding the New Testament, especially Revelations. Those who accept the inspired nature of Daniel delight in its prophetic window into the future.

On the other side of the question, academic scholars reject the inspired nature of Daniel. They cite many historical, archaeological, and linguistic problems which force them to conclude that the Book of Daniel was not written by Daniel himself. They assert that the book is "pseudepigraphal," a book written in the name of a prophet, but not by the prophet himself. They also claim that the book was written many centuries later than the period of its setting.

Basically stated, they believe the Book of Daniel is an inspiring book, but not an inspired one. They discount the possibility of the predictions being the result of revelation. They see the book as an historical narrative written to give the Jewish nation hope during a desperate time. They contend that there was no Daniel at all, much less a book containing revelations given to him.

There is also a difference between how believers themselves see Daniel and its related stories. Catholics and Protestants have different beliefs regarding the book. For example, the Catholic Vulgate Bible has fourteen chapters instead of twelve, as in the King James and other Protestant Bibles. Chapter Thirteen of the Vulgate is known as "Susanna," and Chapter Fourteen is known as "Bel and the Dragon." There has been considerable disagreement over which books belong in Daniel, a problem which is still not fully resolved.

This is not a new problem. Jewish scholars faced the same questions at many points in their history. They met in the first century after Christ to decide which books they could all accept as scripture. Prior to that time, there were many different scriptural traditions. The Dead Sea Scrolls show us that the Qumran Community dealt with this problem as well, since there are different texts, as well different versions and different languages of the same texts. It's not even certain which were considered scriptural by that community and which were not.

It is important to mention from the beginning, that all ancient religious scholars seemed to include Daniel among their books of canon – scripture. While there may be disagreements among different religions regarding the composition of the Book of Daniel, Christians and Jews alike accept the volume as scripture, and always have.

After the crucifixion of Christ, something unforeseen by Judah's Roman rulers occurred. The number of people who accepted Jesus as the Son of God, Savior of mankind, continued to grow. The Jews were already reviled in civilized and learned circles, and the growing Christian movement did not improve their perception. The Christians were viewed as "younger cousins" to the Jewish nation, and were looked down upon with equal contempt. Quickly there grew an effort to ridicule and discredit this growing movement. The Book of Daniel soon became a target for this ridicule.

In the third century A.D., a Neo-Platonist philosopher named Porphyry began to attack the Book of Daniel. Porphyry claimed that it was a work of historical fiction, and listed several 'proofs' to illustrate that fact. That criticism has not only continued, but has grown. For centuries, literary and scientific advancements only worked to prove that Daniel was not the result of revelation, that its date of authorship was much later than the one it claimed. Most concluded that Daniel was actually written during the second century before Christ not the sixth. Study of the book, relying on specific events it describes, was actually able to identify the assumed date of authorship within a very few years.

The experts and scholars have spoken. Daniel is a work of fiction, author unknown, written about 166 B.C. The question had been resolved, it was now time everyone to move on.

No. It's time to look again.

The critical, intellectual study of Daniel begins with Porphyry and his one guiding assumption – there is no such thing as prophesy. Once the researcher accepts this, they are able to place all of the facts into their "proper" context. In the academic world, this assumption is still a fundamental element in the study of Daniel. There is no such thing as prophecy.

I did not begin with that hypothesis. First, an independent study can't begin with a conclusion established. That introduces a real danger that important information will be overlooked if it falls outside of that assumption. Second, despite the preponderance of scientific evidence, in my heart I still believed that the Book of Daniel was exactly what it claimed to be – revelation from God.

So, this turned out to be a contest between my heart and my head.

Statement of the Problem

The question I seek to answer in this study is simple. Is the *Book of Daniel* a work of historical fiction, written by an as yet unknown resident of Palestine at or near the "late date" of 165 B.C.? Or, as the book itself suggests, is the *Book of Daniel* the work of the prophet Daniel, written in Babylon at the "early date," in the middle of the sixth-century B.C.?

These are the two dates suggested for the writing of Daniel. The early date, about 600 B.C., or early date. This date is supported by most religious scholars. The late date, 167 – 165 B.C., which is supported by most in the academic community. Specifically, this work will focus on the "late date," since that is the prevailing scholarly consensus.

More specifically, the problem can be broken down into the following questions:

1) What are the exact arguments made to support a late date, the idea that the book was written during the second-century B.C.?
2) How valid are these arguments?
3) Are there other explanations for these arguments that could influence the assigning of a date of authorship?
4) Are there other factors that may have been overlooked or ignored by those arguing for the second-century date?

Obviously, there is also one other, final issue. Once we have answered the four questions listed above, we have to decide "How will these answers effect our judgment of which date best fits our findings?"

Personally, I think this is an important subject for three reasons. First, the Book of Daniel continues to be part of the battleground between those who believe the Bible is an important book of historical literature, and those who believe the Bible is the Word of God.

Second, this work may help to clarify the differences between the above two groups and opinions of Daniel.

Third, if an argument can be made that evidence for the sixth-century B.C. date exists, it will not only effect the argument for the value of the Bible, but the entire nature of God and his relationship with man.

Definition of Terms

I will at times use terms which may be unfamiliar to some readers, or use words or expressions in a new way. Two examples have already occurred. We have discussed the two different ideas on when the book was written. The "early date" theory of authorship says Daniel was written in the sixth-century B.C., and the "late date" says it was written about 166 B.C.

For this reason, I have included a Glossary at the end of this book. The Glossary will hopefully explain a majority of the new terms that may be encountered. I might even suggest that the reader take a few minutes and review the Glossary now, so they can familiarize themselves with any new terms before hand.

Limitations of the Book

I tried to verify all the information I used throughout this book. Unfortunately, there are some areas where that was not entirely possible. In some instances, I didn't have access to the original information, in other cases I don't have the expertise to render a truly informed judgment upon the findings of cited experts.

One example of this is in the area of linguistics. The study of the Book of Daniel involves detailed research into ancient languages such as Greek, Hebrew and Aramaic. I don't have the training to render a truly knowledgeable evaluation of this linguistic data. In such instances, I rely on published information by the most respected experts I could find.

Another problem is that the body of knowledge continues to expand. Information on the Dead Sea Scrolls, for example, continues to grow. While I have not seen anything that contradicts my previous research, I cannot claim that other, important information has not been uncovered.

Final Comments

I want to offer a disclaimer before we begin. I have tried to be objective, but in the interest of full disclosure, I have to restate that my personal belief tends toward the traditional. I believe than an early date of authorship is the most reasonable. Therefore, I believe that the stories in the *Book of Daniel* are the result of the interaction between God and the prophet Daniel, and not the clever use of history to teach a moral lesson.

Again, I tried to remain as impartial as possible within the scope of the study. However, each reader will have to make their own evaluation regarding my success in doing that.

I should also point out that unless otherwise noted, scriptures cited will be from the Authorized King James Version of the Bible. The KJV is not only my preferred translation, but appears to be the version most used by the experts studied.

CHAPTER 2

Outline of the Book of Daniel

There are several different themes within the book of Daniel. Viewed as a whole, however, the book seeks to demonstrate that the God of Israel is actually the God of all nations. All nations have a place and function in God's plan, but they will nevertheless all pass away when God's kingdom is finally established. Another difference between God's kingdom and the governments of men is that God's kingdom is eternal, and can never be destroyed or supplanted. The book of Daniel provides a prophetic outline of mankind's future from the Babylonian period until this end of times. Since the Book of Daniel is equally important to both the Christian and Jewish faiths, the end of times can be seen as either the Coming of the Messiah, or the Second Coming of Christ.

This outline will quickly look ahead to each chapter, give an overview of the principal theme of each, and its place in the overall organization of the book:

Chapter 1 - This chapter provides an introduction for the book as a whole. It tells of Nebuchadnezzar's capture of Jerusalem, the event which sets in motion all of those which were to follow. This chapter presents the conscription of four young Jewish boys into service to the Chaldeans, and their years of training for service as administrators in the Babylonian Empire. The principal themes in this chapter are:

- The importance of keeping God's covenant, demonstrated here through the refusal to eat from the king's table. The king would have had meat and wine dedicated to the pagan gods served at his table, and by choosing to eat vegetables, they were sure of not partaking in any forbidden foods.
- God rewards those who obey Him. The four youths were blessed as a result of their obedience, and were found to be superior in every way to their fellow candidates.

Chapter 2 – This chapter relates the story of Nebuchadnezzar's first dream. The king is bothered by a dream which he finds disturbing, but which he cannot remember. He calls his advisors and wise men, and tells them to interpret his dream or they will be killed. Daniel eventually reveals the dream to Nebuchadnezzar, and interprets the statue and stone of the dream as the kingdoms of the world and the kingdom of God. The important themes in this chapter are:

- The wisdom of God exceeds the wisdom of man's false gods and those who serve them. Daniel interprets the dream only after the priests and magicians have had an opportunity to perform the task and have failed. The failure of the other gods only serves to highlight the power of Daniel's God.
- The God of Israel is the God of all men. By selecting Nebuchadnezzar to receive the dream, God is proving that He is over all men, even the greatest and most powerful. Nebuchadnezzar is powerless to remember or understand this dream without God's

intervention.
- God has a plan for the world. This fact is established in that this dream reveals a statue, which foretells human events to their end. Its prophetic nature demonstrates God's sovereignty, and his control over mankind. He already knows man's fate, and those steps which will take mankind there.
- God's kingdom will replace the governments of men. All the power of man will be destroyed by the forces put in motion by God, which is represented by a stone cut from a mountain which destroys the statue.

Chapter 3 – In this chapter Daniel's companions, Shadrach, Meshach and Abed-nego, refuse to worship a statue erected by Nebuchadnezzar. They are accused by their enemies of refusing to obey the king's command, and are subsequently thrown into a furnace to be consumed. God intervenes to save them, and Nebuchadnezzar is forced to recognize the power of their God. The important themes in this chapter are:
- Idolatry is a violation of God's law. Throughout Israel's history, the people have struggled with this problem. Today men worship power, money, fame, cars, etc. which have replaced the images of metal and stone as objects of worship.
- It is better to suffer the punishment of men than to disobey God's wishes. These three men all decided that they would rather be put to death than obey the king's direct command to worship a statue.
- God will deliver those who obey him. The king tried to exact his punishment on them, but they were preserved by their God.

Chapter 4 – This chapter is presented as a letter by Nebuchadnezzar to his subjects. It relates the experience of Nebuchadnezzar being punished and then restored by the "Most High God" of Israel. The king is shown the dream of a great tree which covers and protects the creatures of the earth. It is then commanded that the tree be cut down, but that a stump remain which is bound by a metal ring. Nebuchadnezzar was to become like the beats of the field for "seven times" so that he would recognize that God is over all things. Daniel reluctantly interprets the dream for the king. The important themes in this chapter are:

- Earth's rulers govern at the discretion of God. Even the greatest rulers do not control their own destinies, and can be removed when God feels it necessary. The tree gave food and shelter to all, but was cut down immediately when the command was given to do so.
- We should declare God's word no matter what the potential consequences. Daniel certainly had to be concerned that his interpretation regarding the punishment to befall Nebuchadnezzar could bring retribution from the king. Nevertheless, he faithfully declared Gods intentions, ignoring any possible personal cost.
- That boasting in our own power can bring chastisement from God. Nebuchadnezzar was not punished until he proclaimed his own power and accomplishments.
- God is merciful to those who accept him. Nebuchadnezzar finally lifted his eyes to heaven and recognized the power of God over all things. At this point, his reason returned and all of his former glory, and probably more, was returned to him.

Chapter 5 – This chapter introduces us to Belshazzar, who is acting king in the city of Babylon. He attempts to impress his party guests by bringing out the sacred cups

and vessels from the temple at Jerusalem and use them in what is probably a feast involving pagan worship. During this feast, a hand appears, and writes a message on the wall of the room where they are celebrating. None of the other wise men can read the message, and Belshazzar promises great rewards for anyone able to translate the writing. The queen, possibly his mother, tells him of Daniel and his ability to reveal hidden things. Belshazzar calls for Daniel, who does interpret the words and foretells the downfall of Babylon. Babylon indeed falls that very night. The important themes in this chapter are:
- God and his sacred things will not be defiled. By his sacrilege with the sacred temple vessels, Belshazzar earns the anger of God. We must also be careful to respect those things which are God's.
- God's judgments can be swift and final. The punishment promised by God to Belshazzar was final and delivered that very night.

Chapter 6 – This chapter contains the story of Daniel in the lion's den, which is certainly one of the best-known stories in the Bible. Daniel is given a very important position of leadership in the recently conquered Babylon, which creates a great deal of envy among the other governors of the land. Since Daniel is honorable and upright in every aspect of his life, his enemies devise a plan to trap Daniel through his faithfulness to God. Darius is tricked into making a decree that for thirty days all prayers and sacrifices must be directed to him, the king.

Daniel violates this edict, and is punished by being placed in a den of hungry lions. God seals the mouths of the lions, and when Darius returns and finds Daniel unharmed, Darius then throws the accusers and their families in the den. The important themes in this chapter are:
- God's people should be faithful to their

beliefs even when they may bring dire consequences. Daniel knew what would happen if he continued to pray in violation of the king's command, but did so anyway. Daniel could have prayed in an unseen location, avoiding this confrontation, because he probably realized that the edict was designed to entrap him. However, Daniel was faithful.
- God will deliver those who faithfully serve and obey him. Daniel knew what the punishment would be, but placed his faith above his safety. He may not have known whether God would deliver him, but that made no difference in his commitment to God. Daniel was miraculously saved because of his faith.
- God will punish those who oppose His will and attempt to destroy his people. The leaders who had suggested this plan to trap Daniel, then used it in an attempt to have him killed, were in turn destroyed by their own devious plan.

Chapter 7 – This chapter begins the "apocalyptic" section of the book, and takes place in Belshazzar's first year. In the first of Daniel's visions, he sees four beasts representing four kingdoms. These four beasts parallel the four sections of the idol in Chapter Two, only more detail is given. The fourth beast has ten horns, which represent ten kings. After the ten kings, comes a little horn, which makes war with the Saints and prevails. Finally, God creates an eternal kingdom which does away with the kingdoms of the world. This kingdom is given to a Figure like a Son of Man and His Saints. The important themes in this chapter are:
- The future of man. While the interpretations of the imagery in this chapter are unique and varied in nature and detail, almost all

interpreters of this chapter agree that it predicts the path of man's progress until the point where God establishes his kingdom.
- God will assert His right as King to establish His government and rule over the earth. His saints will participate in this eternal kingdom, showing that God rewards those who serve Him.

Chapter 8- This chapter goes into greater detail regarding two of the kingdoms mentioned in Ch's. 2 and 7. The first is the Persian/Median kingdom, which is illustrated by a ram with two horns representing this kingdom. The second kingdom is the Greek kingdom represented by a he-goat with a single, large horn which then destroys the first kingdom.

The single horn (Alexander the Great) is replaced by four horns, which represent the divisions of Alexander's kingdom after his death. There arises a little horn, which casts down some of the hosts of heaven and suspends sacrifice the sanctuary. The little horn is usually associated with Antiochus Epiphanes and the sanctuary is thought to represent the temple. This chapter also talks about the end of times, and a king who will oppose the Prince of princes and be subsequently destroyed. The important themes in this chapter are:
- The history of the world leading up to the coming of the Messiah. Details about attempts to do away with Jewish religious practices are especially significant.
- This chapter also emphasizes that God will ultimately destroy His enemies and restore his people.

Chapter 9 – This chapter contains Daniel's confession and prayer for Jerusalem. Daniel has read the prophecies of Jeremiah and realizes that Jerusalem will be rebuilt. The prayer in this chapter concentrates on

Israel, and her failure to follow God's Word. The end of the chapter talks about the future, from the rebuilding of Jerusalem, to the Messiah and the destruction of Jerusalem and the temple, to the wars leading up to the end. The important themes in this chapter are:

- The coming end of the 70 years. Daniel has read the prophecy of Jeremiah and is able to estimate that the end of the exile should come soon. Daniel's prayer for mercy and forgiveness has the rebuilding of Jerusalem and the Temple in mind.
- Daniel foretells the coming of the Messiah and that Jerusalem, and the Temple will again be destroyed soon after His death. Many experts have alternate interpretations of this chapter, applying it to the times of Antiochus.
- The covenant of God with His people will be confirmed during the period where there are no sacrifices in the Temple.

Chapter 10 – This chapter acts as an introduction to the revelations which follow in chapters 11 and 12. This chapter provides the time, manner and method of communicating the prophecies in the next chapters.

Chapter 11 – This chapter begins Daniel's final revelation. This prophecy provides a detailed look into the future, as opposed to the symbolic references to beasts and the statue made in prior prophecies and interpretations.

While I will avoid commenting on specific interpretations of this chapter, I will make the following observation. Critics emphasize that the description of events here, attributed to the time of Antiochus, are very detailed. They insist that this level of accuracy is proof of the "late date" of authorship, but this detail could simply be the case because of their significance. This period in history would have been the last

opportunity for evil to end the relationship of the Jewish people with their God and the Temple before Christ's coming, which would fulfill the prophecy of Daniel. The important themes in this chapter are:
- The reader receives a description of events and rulers leading up to the day of Antiochus Epiphanes.
- An account of the activities of Antiochus is detailed, leading up to his attempt to pollute the Jewish nation and its religion. Specifically, the attempt to end the ceremonies centered around the Temple.
- The revelation here provides a glimpse into the future. There are several compelling arguments indicating that, starting with vs. 36, the subject shifts from Antiochus to the future Antichrist.

Chapter 12 – This chapter provides an ending to the revelations which preceded it. It predicts a period of tribulation, which will be followed by the general resurrection. God will provide life out of death, and good out of evil.

A timeframe is given for the completion of these events. The actual chronology is not specific, and literally thousands of different interpretations have been offered regarding the specific application of these and other verses to past, present, and future event. God commands finally Daniel to seal up the book until the "time of the end." The important themes in this chapter are:
- The periods of time and events preceding the end of times.
- The two resurrections are introduced. Both the just and the wicked will be resurrected, but to different ends.

Historical Summary

Our study of the Book of Daniel will be enhanced by an understanding of the historical events related to the book, and the events and prophecies given in the book. This section will provide the needed historical framework to do this. It will begin with conditions leading up to the creation of the Neo-Babylonian Empire, and end with the destruction of the Jewish temple by the Romans in about 70 A.D.

The period of rule from the city of Babylon, as related in Daniel, is known as the Neo-Babylonian period. Centuries before this, however, Babylon had been an important center of government, and the empire created by such monarchs as Hammurabi had once established Babylon as the center of a true empire. However, the Assyrians and others over the years had also created other empires, which ruled from different cities.

Immediately before the period detailed in the Book of Daniel, the Assyrians ruled their empire from the city of Nineveh. Internal dissention and pressure from the combined forces of Babylon and Medea led to the fall of Nineveh, and forced the Assyrians to form an alliance with Egypt.

In 605 B.C. the combined Assyrian/Egyptian army made a stand near the city of Carchemish, but were crushed by the Babylonians under the command of crown-prince Nebuchadnezzar. The Babylonian army chased the Egyptians back to their own lands, but the Babylonian king died at this time, and Nebuchadnezzar returned home to assume the throne. It was at this time that the Book of Daniel begins, relating the story of Daniel and several other young men who were taken back to Babylon as noble hostages.

King Nebuchadnezzar died in 562 B.C. and his son Amel Marduk became king. There followed deaths and murders of Babylonian rulers until Nabonidus, a nobleman and husband of Nebuchadnezzar's daughter

Nitocris, became the consensus king of the Babylonian Empire. He soon fell out of favor and left the city of Babylon, not returning until the city was conquered by Cyrus in 539.

Cyrus was the first ruler of the Persian/Median Empire, which expanded to include much of the land between the Mediterranean and modern India. The Persian Empire fought several wars with the Greek states, and was itself destroyed by Alexander the Great. Alexander died in 323 B.C., and his empire was then divided into three. The Egyptian lands were ruled by the Ptolemy dynasty, the Middle East was claimed by Seleucus, and the rest fell to Antigonus.

These three kingdoms fell into frequent conflict over land, often Judah. About 170 B.C. one of the Seleucid rulers made a determined effort to destroy the Jewish culture and religion. This prompted the Maccabees to lead a Jewish revolt. they managed to secure a brief period of independence for Judah. All hope for a Jewish nation vanished when the Roman Empire arrived.

A more detailed history can be found in the Appendix, including a king's list of both the Ptolemy and Seleucid nations.

CHAPTER 3

Section 1: Introduction

In this chapter, we will discuss in detail the various arguments concerning Daniel. This will be done by dividing the discussion into different sections, each focused on a specific area of debate. I will introduced each point, usually by presenting the disputed reference from Daniel, and then the criticisms will be presented and commented upon.

The first topic discussed in section two is known as "the unity of the book." This is a logical starting place, because it will in part shape the subsequent discussion. This question revolves around the suggestion that Daniel may be the work of several different authors whose works were combined to form a single book. If this is the case, then the discussion of dating and authorship would differ for each section from the book. Indeed, any discussion of dating and authorship would be impossible without first clearly identifying each separate author and the section they wrote. This would undoubtedly make the task of dating more complicated, if not meaningless.

If, on the other hand, the book can be shown to be the work of a single author, then the question of dating is simplified. We would be able to state that at a specific point in time, all the material in Daniel existed in a known form. It allows us to establish that at a specific point in time, all the material from Daniel was in existence. Then, by demonstrating that different parts of Daniel are interrelated, we could establish that the date for any of the parts of Daniel can be applied to the book as a whole. Having a single date fore the entire book would be important to our study.

The next section will deal with specific historical arguments directed at the book. These are easy to identify as they make direct references to individuals or events. For example, the Book of Daniel identifies Darius the Mede as the ruler of Babylon after the city's fall to Cyrus. Critics contend that Darius the Mede did not exist. Therefore, the arguments over this person deal with specific factors, related to the historical accuracies of a specific individual, and thus to the book itself.

The following section will deal with indirect references, or lack of references, associated with the book. For example, the book of Daniel seems to indicate that Daniel occupied a prominent position within the Babylonian Empire. Critics point out that there are no independent historical references to Daniel and question how this could be, considering his prominence. These questions will not necessarily deal with specific problems, but more with the context in which sections throughout the book were used.

The fourth topic presented will deal with linguistic factors. The book of Daniel has a complicated linguistic construction. There are different sections, which are written in different languages, and the book uses specific words which were borrowed from still other languages. These words and languages can provide clues as to when and how they were actually used.

It is also important to determine how the book of Daniel developed linguistically and historically. The development of a book of literature can sometimes be followed by looking at different historical examples. Especially for a book of scripture, there are specific conditions which must be met before any book can be accepted as the Word of God. Understanding this process of literary development and ultimate acceptance by the community will allow us to estimate how long Daniel had been known and circulated.

Finally, we will attempt to draw conclusions from the material discussed. It will be impossible to establish a conclusive answer to our questions, but we should be able to evaluate the strength or weakness of specific arguments. This will, in turn, allow us to formulate an overall impression of the questions we are evaluating.

Section 2: Unity of the Book

The question "Who wrote the book of Daniel?" has lingered for centuries. In Jewish and Early Christian traditions, it was universally accepted that the prophet Daniel was its sixth-century B.C. author. Doubts arose only later regarding its authenticity, as mentioned earlier, with Porphyry about 300 A.D. His theories were universally opposed by Jewish and Christian scholars and discredited, lay dormant and largely forgotten until the last few centuries. Since then, the study and analysis of Daniel have been a back and forth battle between those who accept the book at face value, and those who reject its early date of origin.

The most common alternative explanation is that a single author, or small group of scholars, wrote the book in the middle of the second-century B.C. There is another theory, however, that must be mentioned. Some believe that Daniel is simply a collection of inspirational stories, of undetermined origin, prepared for the Jews of Palestine. The author of Daniel simply collected these stories, combined them, and published them in the name of a previously unknown prophet. If Daniel is a collection of unrelated stories, this will make a study of it's authorship difficult, if not impossible.

Current scholarship, fortunately, has weighed in regarding the authorship of the original Hebrew version of the book, and there is unanimity regarding at least one aspect of the question of authorship. Most scholars now agree that the book of Daniel is the result of a single author and not a group of writers working together. The Anchor Bible commentary on Daniel states:

> There are certain features in the book which seem to point to one author or at most two for the whole work. Every section of the book lays special emphasis on the belief that the God of Israel is master and guide of human history; that he knows the future and reveals its secrets to his chosen ones, and that under his rule the kingdom of his holy people will ultimately supplant the pagan empires of the world.[1]

There are a number of reasons for assuming it was the work of a single author. Cyrus Gordon arrived at this conclusion based on the structure of the book:

> Hammurabi's Code has a comprehensive literary form. The prologue and epilogue are in poetry, who's form is parallelistic and whose language is archaic. The laws in the middle, however, are in prose, so that the whole composition has a pattern, which we call ABA. . . . Similarly the biblical Book of Daniel begins and ends in Hebrew, though the middle is in Aramaic. The possibility of an intentional ABA structure deserves earnest consideration

and should deter us from hastily dissecting the text.²

Gordon believes the structure illustrates an old and popular form of composition which was very common in the ancient near east.

We know that the book was written in two languages, Hebrew and Aramaic. The fact that there are linguistic differences does not detract from the overall unity of the book, however. Robert Pfeiffer writes:

> It is obvious to all that the Aramaic section (2:4b-7:28) could never have constituted a separate work without the Hebrew section preceding it, or at least without 2:1-4a. Moreover, ch. 7 belongs to the first part according to the language but to the second according to its contents.³

The construction seems to represent an intentional effort to linguistically link the two sections, which are different thematically.

While the idea of textual unity may be interesting, why is it important to the overall analysis of the book of Daniel? The fact that the book of Daniel reflects a carefully crafted work, designed to unify the different sections of the book structurally and linguistically, refutes one of the arguments proposed by critics of the book. It was suggested at one time that the book of Daniel was simply a collection of independently circulating stories. The belief was that these stories, at some later date, were gathered, put together in one volume, and then distributed throughout the Jewish community.

Current studies into the construction of the book of Daniel completely discount this argument. There is currently almost no support at all for this idea. Almost every aspect of the book demonstrates a deliberate and well designed theme and structure, done within the framework an overall plan. The Hebrew version, literarily, cannot be considered anything but a single, finely crafted work.

Therefore, as we analyze the book, we must keep in mind this unity. We cannot arbitrarily separate chapters or sections for individual interpretation. The book must be considered as a unit, because it was planned and created as a unit.

We cannot assert, however, that the form we now have represents exactly the original form of the book. It is impossible for a book to be passed down through time the way the books of scripture were, without suffering changes.

If we compare the Hebrew version with the early Greek Septuagint (LXX) version, differences are immediately found. The organization and expression are not as well developed in the Greek version, but the unity is still there. The LXX is probably compiled from an older text than the version of Daniel in today's scriptures, but many of the arguments regarding unity are still valid even if the presentation of the material was later improved. The packaging was made a little prettier, but the contents remained essentially the same.

We do not have a complete picture of the process by which the original works were preserved and passed down. We do suggest, nevertheless, that efforts to separate the individual sections should be resisted. Joyce Baldwin quotes the scholar H. H. Rowley:

> Rowley's forceful conclusion still stands: 'the onus of proof lies upon those who would dissect a work. Here, however, nothing that can be seriously called proof of compositeness has been produced. On the other hand evidence for the unity of the work that in its totality amounts to a demonstration is available.'   [quoting

from a paper by H. H. Rowley entitled 'The Unity of the Book of Daniel', read as a Presidential Address to the Society for Old Testament Study in 1950, Published in 'The Servant of the Lord' (Oxford, 1965), pp. 249-280.]4

Our analysis of the historical parts of the book, therefore, will reflect on the authority of the book as a whole. As we examine the arguments for and against the competing theories of authorship, they must then be applied to the book as a whole. We cannot allow the acceptance of the historical parts, while rejecting the prophetic.

Section 3: Direct Historical Arguments

Briefly stated, proponents of a second-century B.C. date for Daniel claim that direct and indirect historical references confirm the author had only a limited knowledge of historical events during the time in which the book claims to have been written. As Robert H. Pfieffer simply states regarding the history in Daniel, "The information for the periods preceding Alexander [356-323B.C.] is sketchy and erroneous." [5] The implication is that if Daniel had actually been alive during the period in question, several elements within the text would be different.

The late Cyrus H. Gordon, whose candid studies of Bible History and Archaeology are well-known and respected, was less circumspect:

> The book contains such grotesque errors concerning the Neo-Babylonian and Achaemenian empires that as a historic source for those periods Daniel is of quite limited value. One of the *faux pas* is that Belshazzar (erroneously called the son of

> Nebuchadnezzar) was the king of Babylon when Cyrus conquered it. [6]

While the term 'grotesque' may be a bit more colorful than most might have chosen, this sentiment against an early date seems to be the most common in academic circles.

The arguments against an early date assert that historical information becomes more accurate as the historical references approach the second-century B.C., specifically those dealing with the life of Antiochus IV (know as Epiphanes). "The historical surveys given in Chs. 2, 7, and 11 show only vague familiarity with events belonging to the period of the Exile and the early postexilic age; they increase in accuracy and definiteness as they approach the times of the author, and culminate, in each case, with the figure and fate of the Syrian ruler."[7]

While the questions of date and authorship for the book of Daniel are in dispute, the date and authorship for the work which began the criticism of Daniel are not. Doubts about the authenticity of the book of Daniel began with the philosopher Porphyry and his writing in opposition to the growing Christian religion. We find these arguments against Daniel by "the Neoplatonist Porphyry (cerca A.D. 304), preserved in Jerome's commentary on Daniel (c A.D. 400); in the course of his attack on other 'apocalypses,' Porphyry dates the book in the second-century B.C. and terms most of its 'prophecies' *vaticinia ex eventu*."[8] The term *vaticinia ex eventu* means "prophecy after the event," and the term suggests that the events presented in Daniel as prophecy should actually be classified as history.

Porphyry was the first to suggest that the book of Daniel was not what it presented itself to be. Until this time, Jewish and Christian traditions universally agreed that the book was authored by the prophet Daniel himself, no later than the times of Cyrus 'the Persian'. Since Porphyry, *vaticinia ex eventu* is the standard by which Daniel has been measured.

By analyzing the Daniel as history, scholars feel that the date of authorship can be closely estimated:

> The date of the book can be determined quite exactly. The visions all point to the same historical situation: the persecutions of the Jews by Antiochus IV Epiphanes (175-164 B.C.), the king of the Seleucid Empire that emerged from the wars of the Diadochi after the death of Alexander the Great. On the one hand, the author is familiar with the return of Antiochus from his second campaign against Egypt (169 B.C.) and the "abomination that makes desolate" (11:31), the desecration of the Jewish Temple by an altar of Zeus (167 B.C.). On the other hand, he shows no knowledge of Antiochus' death in Persia (December 164).[9]

It must be admitted that evidence supporting a date of composition between 167-164 B.C., at first glance, appears quite compelling. Couple this with the fact that a majority of scholars, academic and religious, agree that the late date is all but certain, and further research may almost seem unnecessary or futile.

Nevertheless, let us begin our study of the text of Daniel. Not surprisingly, we don't have to venture far into the book before the historical criticisms begin, as the first verse of the first chapter offers us several details which are considered mistakes by most scholars.

Criticism #1: Daniel 1:1,2

The Issues:
1 – Did Nebuchadnezzar capture Jerusalem as described here?

2 – If so, when did it happen?
3 – Does Daniel misspell the name of Nebuchadnezzar?

The Verse in Question:

> **1:1, 2 In the third year of the reign of Jehoiakim king of Judah came Nebuchadnezzar king of Babylon unto Jerusalem, and besieged it. And the Lord gave Jehoiakim king of Judah into his hand, with part of the vessels of the house of God: which he carried into the land of Shinar to the house of his God; and he brought the vessels into the treasure house of his God.**

The very first statement in Daniel introduces the relationship between the 'third year of Jehoiakim' and Nebuchadnezzar. If you will recall from the earlier section dealing with the history of this region that in the year 605 B.C. Nebuchadnezzar, still crown prince, defeated the army of Necho and broke the Egyptian domination of Syria and Palestine. This event is also recorded in Jeremiah 46:2 "**Against Egypt, against the army of Pharaohnecho king of Egypt, which was by the river Euphrates in Carchemish, which Nebuchadrezzar king of Babylon smote in the fourth year of Jehoiakim the son of Josiah, King of Judah.**"

This undoubtedly coincides with the time referred to here by Daniel, but there is a problem. Jeremiah states that this took place in the fourth year of Jehoiakim, not the third – Daniel is in apparent conflict with the earlier book. The critics of Daniel's claim to authorship waste no time in pointing out the conflict:

> The first historical reference (1:1) is incorrect. We know from reliable sources (Kings and Jer.) that Nebuchadnezzar did not take Jerusalem in the third year of Jehoiakim (606) . . . Nebuchadnezzar was not yet "king of Babylon" in Jehoiakim's third year, for he succeeded Nabopolassar in 605, after the victory at Carchemish (cf. Kings 24:7, Jer. 46:2), following which Jehoiakim remained an obedient vassal of Nebuchadnezzar for three years.[10]

It will be better to deal with all of the issues relating to this verse and to the 3rd or 4th year question at this time. In doing so we will first examine whether it was likely, or even possible, for Nebuchadnezzar to have captured Jerusalem at this time. The Abingdon Bible Commentary states, "There is no mention elsewhere of this siege of Jerusalem, and the statement is one of the historical perplexities of the book [of Daniel]."[11]

Once we have established whether the capture of Jerusalem actually occurred, we will move on to the question of in exactly which year this event took place. If we conclude that this event never happened, then any attempt to date the non-existent event will be doubly futile.

Let us review then what is going on at this time. The Assyrian Empire has all but vanished, and Pharaoh Necho belatedly enters the war against the Babylonians on the side of his Assyrian ally. Syria and Palestine are nominally under the control of the Egyptians, but when Necho attempts to advance for the first time through Palestine, he is opposed by King Josiah, who is quickly defeated. Soon there after, Necho places Jehoiakim on the throne because of his loyalty to Egypt.

The Egyptian forces are then finally engaged in a decisive battle at Carchemish, near the Euphrates River and are totally defeated by Nebuchadnezzar. The Egyptians take flight, and as Nebuchadnezzar pursues them back toward Egypt, he receives news that his father has died. He then rushes back to Babylon to participate in the New Year's rites. Philip R. Davies summarized the problem nicely: "In actual fact, the third year of Jehoiakim was 606, before Nebuchadnezzar was 'king of Babylon'. It was also the year in which he conquered the Pharaoh Necho at Carchemish, and a siege of Jerusalem at this time is improbable."[12]

In order to clarify the picture further, let us look at these events, and their dating, a little closer. Here is an interesting summary of these events:

> The Saite Pharaoh Necho joined forces with Ashuruballit and confidently awaited a Babylonian attack near Carchemish. But Nebuchadrezzar, the Babylonian crown prince, crushed the Egyptian-Assyrian host and Necho's survivors fled south, followed by the taunts of the Hebrew prophet Jeremiah. Impressed by the defeat of the Pharaoh, the small powers of Syria and Palestine quickly submitted to the victorious Chaldeans. Nebopolassar had died during the campaign against Necho, and Nebuchadrezzar hurried to Babylon to assume the throne.[13]

A better understanding of the historical timeframe involved is available from Joyce Baldwin, who takes her inform from actual Babylonian inscriptions of that period:

> The following table sets out the details as they can be reconstructed from the Babylonian data for 605 B.C. January/February - Army returned from a campaign to Babylon. April/August

> (probably May/June) Battle of Carchemish, after which Nebuchadrezzar pursued the Egyptians south and conquered the whole of Hatti-land (i.e. Syria-Palestine). August 15-Death of Nabopolassar, father of Nebuchadrezzar. September 7-Assencion of Nebuchadrezzar.[14]

It would appear, then, that the Babylonian records themselves indicate that the land of Palestine, or Hatti, was conquered at this time.

The sequence of events then seems fairly certain; Nebuchadnezzar defeated the Egyptians, and then followed them south – undoubtedly hoping to completely destroy the Egyptian army – until he was called home after the death of his father.

Several new questions arise: 1) did Nebuchadnezzar follow as far as Jerusalem, 2) would he have bothered with Jerusalem at all, and 3) was there enough time for him to have conquered the city?

We will now address these three questions in more detail. First, is there any evidence that Nebuchadnezzar traveled as far as Jerusalem in his pursuit of Necho? In fact, there is evidence that his army may have actually advanced further. *The Oxford History of Ancient Egypt* reports the event as follows:

> "The Egyptians were able to establish themselves on the Euphrates for a short while, but this position was soon lost in 605 BC as a result of their catastrophic reverse at Carchemish, which was followed by a brusque retreat to the eastern frontier of Egypt."[15]

A pursuit to the Egyptian border would require Nebuchadnezzar and his forces to pass well beyond

Palestine and the city of Jerusalem. It is safe to assume that if the Egyptian forces retreated that far, the Babylonian forces would have followed them as far and as fast as possible, even to the borders of Egypt itself.

Since the *Oxford History* would certainly constitute credible evidence that Nebuchadnezzar did continue past Jerusalem, the next question asks whether Nebuchadnezzar would have bothered with the Jews at all. After all, his main objective was the destruction of the Egyptian army.

We must recall that Jehoiakim was placed on the throne at Jerusalem by the Pharaoh Necho himself, and would have to be considered a loyal Egyptian subject by the advancing Babylonians. Even though the Egyptians were in full retreat, it is highly unlikely that the Babylonian army would leave a potential enemy force to its rear, and it is certain that Nebuchadnezzar would not expose his forces to possible attack from behind.

A simple map illustrating the geographic relationships of the places we have discussed can be found on the following page. If you follow the most direct route from Carchemish to Egypt, you notice that the path of both armies would pass too close to Jerusalem for it to be ignored.

Map 1

It was obvious at this point that the Babylonians were victorious, and it was equally certain that Jehoiakim, having just seen the Egyptian army flee helplessly past would not hesitate to shift his allegiance from Egypt to Babylon. There is no reason whatsoever to doubt that Nebuchadnezzar, even if not attending to it in person, would have sent a force to ascertain the threat from the Jewish nation.

It appears that the Jews offered no resistance and were probably quite eager to pledge loyalty to Babylon. Even with that resolved, Judah had been a vassal state of Egypt and had just become a vassal of Babylon. It would be very strange indeed if the some form of tribute were not exacted by Nebuchadnezzar and his army.

A point of clarification must be established before proceeding. The Book of Daniel does not assert that Jerusalem was destroyed at this time, and in fact it was not. Some critics have carelessly tried to link these two unrelated events.

> Second Kings 24:6 merely says that Jehoiakim "slept with his fathers and Jehoiachin his son reigned in his stead," after which the chapter describes Jehoiachin's surrender to Nebuchadnezzar, who then carried him, the royal family, and other "chief men of the land" to Babylon. So both biblical and Babylonian records indicate that Jerusalem fell to Nebuchadnezzar in the last year of Jehoiakim's reign and not in his third year as the writer of Daniel indicated.[16]

At no point in these verses of Daniel does it state, or even imply, that the city of Jerusalem was destroyed, or that the king was carried off into captivity. A measure of tribute from the temple may have been required, but that hardly qualifies as the type of conquest implied in the criticism above. And while it is true, if not likely, that some people may have been taken to Babylon, those taken back were not necessarily slaves, but probably what is considered noble hostages. Members of a nations ruling class brought to the capital for education, and often as candidates for administrative service in the Babylonian empire. And if the vassal nation rebelled, it endangered the lives of the hostages.

A much more reasonable, though equally skeptical attitude was expressed by S. R. Driver. Driver is responsible for some of the classic statements in opposition to a sixth-century date for Daniel and will be cited again, but regarding this particular topic he states:

> That Nebuchadnezzar besieged Jerusalem, and carried away some of the sacred vessels in "the Third year of Jehoiakim" (Dan 1:1f), though it cannot, strictly speaking, be disproved, is highly improbable: not only is the Book of Kings silent, but Jeremiah *in the following year* (c 25, & c.: see v.1), speaks of the Chaldaeans in a manner which appears distinctly to imply that their arms had not yet been seen in Judah.[17]

Jeremiah, in fact, does state that Nebuchadrezzar will fulfill God's will by destroying the Jewish nation, but there is absolutely no indication that the Chaldeans could not have been there before. The Babylonian Army would not attack Jerusalem if their main force was committed to pursuing the Egyptians, and the Jew posed no immediate threat.

I suggest that the surrender of Jerusalem at this specific time cannot be proven or disproven, as Driver indicates. Keeping in mind there is evidence to indicate that Nebuchadnezzar would have had to pass near Jerusalem to follow the Egyptians in their "retreat to the eastern frontier of Egypt." Also, with the idea that he would simply ignore the possible threat of the Kingdom of Judah being unlikely, there is enough evidence for the historical accuracy of Daniel's account being possible to consider it further.

Now our second question, when did this occur? The Book of Daniel states that this happened in "the third year of the reign of Jehoiakim." Most scholars consider this a clear indication that the author of Daniel was not familiar with the event, since in Jeremiah 46: 2 it states: "Against Egypt, against the army of Pharaohnecho king of Egypt, which was by the river Euphrates in Carchemish, which Nebuchadrezzar king of Babylon smote in the fourth year of Jehoiakim the son of Josiah king of Judah."

The conflict appears to be obvious. Jeremiah claims it happened in the fourth year, Daniel in the third. One is right, the other is wrong.

Actually, this is not the case. The Jews had two calendars, one religious and the other civil. The religious calendar, certainly used by the prophet Jeremiah, began at the Passover, celebrated during the month of Nisan (April). The religious calendar concentrated mainly on the spiritual observances of the Jewish people. The battle of Carchemish occurred during the summer of 605 B.C., several months after the beginning of the religious new year, making it the fourth year of the reign of Jehoiakim rule.

The second calendar used by the Jews at this time was the civil calendar, used in governmental affairs. This calendar begins with the new year holiday of Rosh Hashana, which begins the month of Tishri (October). The battle of Carchemish occurred before the beginning of the civil new year, making it the third year of the reign of Jehoiakim by the governmental dating method.

Here again, I find the arguments of the critics of

Daniel a bit confusing. They claim the book was written by a scholar in the centuries before the birth of Christ. Yet, they are willing to accept that this scholar was unaware of, or willfully ignored, the writing of Jeremiah concerning this event. Why would someone who must rely solely on available historical sources be so willing to contradict what is a commonly accepted historical fact? If it had been written by someone with only an intimate knowledge Jeremiah, they would have placed it in the same year as that prophet. Again, the text of Daniel proves more plausible than its critics.

At this point, neither the first nor second questions regarding the capture of Jerusalem by Nebuchadnezzar are completely resolved. If the Babylonian and Egyptian histories are to be believed, however, we must concede that the evidence lends equal, if not greater, support to the scenario represented in Daniel than to those suggested by its critics. The suggested contradiction of Daniel dating of the event by Jeremiah is adequately explained. There is certainly enough evidence, therefore, to justify our continued investigation into the third question.

The question of whether there was enough time for Nebuchadnezzar to have accomplished the conquest of Jerusalem before returning to Babylon, will not be discussed in as much detail as the previous two. I was unable to find any authoritative statements regarding a required time for its accomplishment. Although many expressed firm opinions on this subject, the speculations by various experts seemed to correspond closely to their stated opinions regarding the subject of in general. If they support the authenticity of Daniel, they saw no major difficulty in the conquest being conducted during this period - those critical of the book disagreed.

However, I feel quite confident in stating that within the framework of our previous assertions – a headlong retreat by the Egyptians and an equally swift pursuit by Nebuchadnezzar – a conquest of Jerusalem cannot be discounted. A good field general, once his enemy's organization has collapsed, would move as quickly as possible to maintain contact and press the advantage. A period of two or three months would allow more than enough time for the Babylonian forces to advance through Palestine "to the eastern frontier of Egypt."

Daniel's account is in no way contradicted by the existing evidence. In fact, the evidence may suggest Daniel's is a more realistic description that those of its critics. Nebuchadnezzar had the means, reason and time to have captured Jerusalem after the battle of Carchemish.

The third point of conflict, albeit a minor one, is also found in the first verse of Daniel. It involves the spelling of the name Nebuchadnezzar itself. Some critics contend that the way in which the book of Daniel spells Nebuchadnezzar's name indicates that the author was unfamiliar with it. The verse from Jeremiah quoted above uses the name "Nebuchadrezzar," which may experts argue is the correct spelling. The Babylonian spelling of the name is *Nebuchadrezzar*, the "r" in the middle of the name instead of an "n". The Abingdon Bible Commentary explains:

> *Nebuchadnezzar* -- an incorrect spelling of "Nebuchadrezzar," the form which appears *generally* (italics added) in Jeremiah and Ezekiel, the prophets who were contemporaries of the king.[18]

Since the author of this commentary has already decided that Daniel was the work of a second-century B.C. writer, any difference is immediately attributed to that cause. The way the information is phrased, explaining that Jeremiah and Ezekiel used Nebuchadrezzar because they were "the prophets who were contemporaries of the king," implies that Daniel was not. The actual statement of many critics specifies that the spelling of the name Nebuchadrezzar "generally" appears in these books, and we will delve into this qualification in more detail a little later.

A few critics even have an interesting explanation suggested for the change:

> The name Nebuchadnezzar contains a disguised reference to Antiochus to those acquainted with Hebrew numbering. The Babylonian king of 605-562 BCE was in fact called Nabu-kuddurri-usur which should be transliterated into Hebrew script as NeuchadRezzar [Nebuchadrezzar] (as it is in e.g. Jeremiah 46:2, 39:11). The change of that one letter gives this name the same numerical value in Hebrew (which had no separate numbers and soused letters to represent numbers) as the name Antiochus Epiphanes. This is too coincidental to be accidental and to contrived to be miraculous.[19]

It can hardly be contrived if a valid reason can be found for the change. As far as being a coincidence, those are the names – they are fact, not coincidence.

While this is a problem for some of the critics of this Old Testament book, it is interesting that many academic specialists display no reluctance to use the name "Nebuchadnezzar" themselves. Many of the academic, archaeological and historical texts use the name Nebuchadnezzar as the correct form. Here is just one example by Wolfram von Soden, a highly respected German Assyriologist:

> The most significant king of the dynasty was Nebuchadnezzar II (Nabu-kudurru-

ussur; 605-562), who generally maintained peace with the Medes."[20]

There is an almost endless supply of examples from scholars of every discipline to confirm the common use of Nebuchadnezzar as an acceptable use and translation of the king's name.

Despite the wide spread academic acceptance of the name, if there were no compelling explanation for this change, it may still leave some question as to why Daniel chose to use it. However, there are some very reasonable explanations for the change. The International Standard Bible Encyclopedia states:

1. This change from "r" to "n" which is found in the two writings of the name in the Hebrew and the Aramaic of the Scriptures is a not uncommon one in the Semitic languages, as in Burnaburiyash and Burraburiyash, Ben-hadad and Bar-hadad (see Brockelmann's Comparative Grammar, 136, 173, 220).

There is, therefore, evidence that the different names are simply reflecting common differences in the Aramaic and Hebrew languages.

Another, equally interesting explanation relates to different dialects used at that time in the Babylonian Empire. It has been suggested that one usage reflects the Babylonian version of the name, while the other reflects the Aramaic translation.

> It is possible, however, that the form Nebuchadnezzar is the Aramaic translation of the Babylonian Nebuchadrezzar. If we take the name to be compounded of Nabu-kudurri-usur in the sense "O Nebo, protect thy servant,"

then Nabu-kedina-usur would be the best translation possible in Aramaic.

I would also like to examine this argument within the main critical framework of this thesis. It is my contention that the detailed study of this question, and subsequent arguments regarding the accuracy and historical validity of Daniel, was not used by critics as the basis for arriving at any conclusions regarding the book. Quite the opposite, the academically established conclusion - that the Book of Daniel could not have been written by the historically accepted author - was instead the basis by which all the evidence was evaluated.

It is now commonly assumed that the book could not have been written during the time of its setting. To the academic and scientific worlds and their demands for proof, it is almost a given that no one could have predicted future events with the degree of accuracy evident in Daniel. Therefore, the individual facts have to be interpreted within the established fact of the books second century composition.

Applying this fact to our continuing discussion of the name Nebuchadnezzar, we previously pointed out that the critics placed a qualification on the use of the name Nebuchadrezzar in the Bible. They state that with regards to the spelling question, the term "generally" applies. Another example of a critic's use of this qualifier is found in *A Commentary on the Holy Bible* which makes the following comment:

> The name of the Babylonian conqueror of Jerusalem is always spelt in Daniel as Nebuchadnezzar, while contemporary writers like Jeremiah and Ezekiel *generally* (italics again added) give the correct form Nebuchadrezzar.[21]

I find this, and all similar statements, to be somewhat misleading. A review of *Strong's Exhaustive Concordance of the Bible* shows that in terms of total usage, the term Nebuchadnezzar is used more often in the Bible itself than the alternative – and supposedly correct - spelling. Even after eliminating all of the references in Daniel from the count, the term Nebuchadrezzar is used 31 times, while the name Nebuchadnezzar is used 28 times by other biblical sources. This hardly reflects a major difference.[22]

There are other considerations regarding the two names. The name of Nebuchadrezzar is found in two books, Jeremiah and Ezekiel. The name Nebuchadnezzar is found in seven books other than Daniel: 2 Kings, 1 & 2 Chronicles, Ezra, Nehemiah, Esther, and Jeremiah. Jeremiah can hardly be considered a witness to the name "Nebuchadnezzar" being incorrectly used in Daniel, when that same (supposedly incorrect) name is found ten times in his own writings.

Now consider the fact that Daniel would have written his record later in life, after having spent much of his life as an official in the Babylonian government. Aramaic would have been the language of his work and daily life. The fact that he chose to use the Aramaic version of his name should be considered a supporting argument instead of a criticism.

This specific criticism of the Book of Daniel would never have been suggested if the late date of authorship were not a foregone conclusion. In fact, on its own merits, the use of the name Nebuchadnezzar seems to be the more accepted of the two.

Issues from Criticism #1– In Conclusion:
1 – Did Nebuchadnezzar capture Jerusalem as described here? While there is no definitive statement regarding Nebuchadnezzar's actions toward Jerusalem, there is credible historical evidence that his army did pass through Judah at this exact time. This

would make it a near certainty that the Babylonian army would have eliminated the Jewish capital as a possible threat. This is much different than his capture of Jerusalem, which occurred later. Critics confuse what are probably two separate events.

2 – If so, when did it happen? It happened in the summer 605 B.C. This was the fourth year of Jehoiakim when measured by the religious calendar, and the third year when measured by the civil calendar.

3 – Does Daniel misspell the name of Nebuchadnezzar? No, he used the very common Aramaic spelling of the name, like many of the other Old Testament prophets.

CRITICISM #2: Daniel 1:3 & 4

The Issues:
1 – Did Daniel misuse the term "Chaldean?"

The Verse in Question:

> **1:3, 4 And the king spake unto Ashpenaz the master of his eunuchs, that he should bring certain of the children of Israel, and of the king's seed, and of the princes; Children in whom was no blemish, but well favored, and skilful in all wisdom, and cunning in knowledge, and understanding science, and such as had ability in them to stand in the king's palace, and whom they might teach the learning and the tongue of the Chaldeans.**

The use of the term Chaldean in the book of Daniel is considered to be almost *prima fascia* evidence of its late date of authorship. The problem rests on Daniel's supposed reference to the Chaldeans as "**the magicians, and the astrologers, and the sorcerers**" (2:2) of the Babylonian Empire. Critics maintain that this connotation for the term was unknown in the 6th century B.C., and that its exclusive meaning was racial at that time.

Pfeiffer illustrates the question:

> Another anachronism in relation to Nebuchadnezzar's reign is the use of "Chaldeans" not in its original sense (an Aramaic tribe in Southern Babylonia from which Nebuchadnezzar's dynasty had sprung) but, as in Greek and Roman authors, in the sense of "astrologers" or "diviners" (1:4; 2:2, etc.)[23]

Those supporting a late date are unanimous in their belief that no one alive during the Neo-Babylonian period would have used the term Chaldean in the way Daniel did.

The question arises, however, as to exactly how the term was used at that time. Those asserting its exclusive application as a racial reference may have a difficult time proving their point. It is true that there are no examples of the term being used to describe the mystics or astrologers in a Babylonian context, but that is probably because "there is a complete absence of the word from Babylonian records of the sixth century in either of its senses."[24] There is no evidence at all regarding the accuracy of Daniel's references, one way or another.

We know who the Chaldeans were, they were the people from Chaldea, a region in southwestern Babylonia. Nebuchadnezzar was himself a Chaldean. It is accepted that the original connotation was ethnic, but considering the lack of direct evidence regarding its usage at that time, one wonders how critics can justify the enormous importance attributed to this argument. Philip R. Davies illustrates this attitude:

> Perhaps the most important evidence, linguistically, against such a date [early date] is the use of the word 'Chaldean' to mean a class of magician in ten of its twelve occurrences in Daniel. Such a usage hardly belongs to the sixth century, when the term was a racial one, denoting the Babylonians. This is its meaning in Kings, Isaiah, Jeremiah, Ezekiel, and Habakkuk and twice in Daniel, at 5.30 and 9.1. This kind of consideration leads to the conclusion that the Aramaic portions of Daniel are not the product of a Babylonian Jew under Nebuchadnezzar or his immediate successors.[25]

There are at least two major flaws in this logic. First, the other Biblical writers were writing from outside the Babylonian/Chaldean culture while Daniel was writing from within. Nebuchadnezzar was a Chaldean, so a racial use of Chaldean would be redundant. We usually refer to ourselves as "Americans" in many specific contexts. One is when we are pointing out a contrast between ourselves and another nationality. "Americans and Canadians have much in common." While these two groups have many traits in common, the nationality must be used when both are present.

Another instance when we are highlighting a specific characteristic associated with our nationality. If someone were to make the comment "Americans are willing to perform their patriotic duties," the meaning would not need clarification. We are not implying that every American performs these duties, but that someone who takes their nationality seriously does. The reference would be used only to provide clarification or emphasis.

This example can also be applied to the term Chaldean. A racial use would not be appropriate because there is no racial contrast needed, and would actually be confusing. Especially when we consider the difficulty in writing at that time, the term would probably be used only when necessary, and then just to provide emphasis or clarification. It would probably never be used as simply a racial reference, and after reviewing several historical accounts, written in Babylon at this time, no references were made at all to the people of Babylon. All inscriptions were designed to relate the activities of the "king of the Babylonians" and not the people.

The second flaw also relates to the racial characteristics referent to the term Chaldean. There is no reason to believe that all of the wise men and magicians were of Chaldean ancestry. In fact, it is extremely unlikely that they were all Chaldeans. The Babylonian Empire was expansive, and included many different lands. It is difficult to believe that all magicians, astrologers, sorcerers, etc. were Chaldean. Most of the Babylonians were not Chaldeans.

This means that the term Chaldean could not be accurately used to describe all people from this class. If you look at Daniel's references to the Chaldeans, they actually suggest they were a distinct group. Looking at Daniel 2:10 it says, "**there is no king, lord, nor ruler, that asked such things at any magician, or astrologer, or Chaldean**." We know that magicians and astrologers are different, so this would indicate that Daniel believes that the Chaldeans are also different than these two groups. If the Chaldeans were of this profession, then Daniel's reference would be applied to those magicians who were of Chaldean descent. If the term Chaldean was used to specify those of this class who were Chaldeans, then the term was indeed used to denote a racial characteristic, and the arguments of the critics are not well thought out and incorrect.

In addition, we must keep in mind that many

believe the date of authorship *was not* during the reign of the Babylonians, but during the period of Persian rule immediately after. Daniel states that he is writing **"In the third year of Cyrus king of Persia"** (10:1), several years after the cities' capture. Perhaps the real question being asked should be, "Is there any indication how the term Chaldean was used in a Persian context after the fall of Babylon?" Fortunately, we do have some direct evidence regarding this question.

Herodotus was a Greek historian in the fifth-century B.C. and was called the father of history. He traveled across the known world and recorded as much of its history as possible, which he entered into his book, entitled simply *History*. He is believed to have visited Persia during the first half of the fifth century, a little more than a half-century after the traditional date suggested for the writing of Daniel. Here is his description of the Chaldeans from Book One of his *History*:

> On the topmost tower there is a spacious temple, and inside the temple stands a couch of unusual size, richly adorned, with a golden table by its side. There is no statue of any kind set up and the native woman, who, as the Chaldaeans, the priests of this god, affirm, is chosen for himself by the deity out of all the women of the land.

Again later:

> The Chaldaeans told me that all the gold together was eight hundred talents' weight. Outside the temple are two altars, one of solid gold, on which it is only lawful to offer sucklings; the other a common altar, but of great size, on which the full-grown animals are sacrificed. It is also on

> the great altar that the Chaldaeans burn the frankincense, which is offered to the amount of a thousand talents' weight, every year, at the festival of the God. In the time of Cyrus there was likewise in this temple a figure of a man, twelve cubits high, entirely of solid gold. I myself did not see this figure, but I relate what the Chaldaeans report concerning it.

Herodotus description of the Chaldeans function in the city of Babylon was to act as intermediaries between the gods and man, and to handle the official religious functions. There can be no question that the description of Herodotus correlates very closely with that of the Chaldeans as recorded in Daniel.

We must also qualify another aspect of the criticism of Daniel's use of the term "Chaldean." One gets the impression from the critics that Daniel was unaware of the fact that the term 'Chaldean' was also used to denote a racial subset of the Babylonians. S. R. Driver insists that "The 'Chaldaeans' are synonymous in Da. 1&2. with the caste of wise men."[26] While this may be true, Daniel does show us he is aware of the other meaning. In at least two places Daniel uses the ethnic meaning. In the fifth chapter, verse thirty he says, "**In that night was Belshazzar the *king of the Chaldeans* slain**." Then in the first verse of chapter nine he explains, "**In the first year of Darius the son of Ahasuerus, of the seed of the Medes, which was made king over *the realm of the Chaldeans***." (italics added)

Daniel was not ignorant of the ethnic meaning of the word Chaldean, he was simply aware of them both. The certainty regarding this question, as expressed by some proponents of the late date, may need to be reexamined.

If we combine the information gathered regarding the Chaldeans, a completely different view begins to emerge. I do not believe the critics of Daniel, or unfortunately its supporters either, have been thorough in their examination of this point. The first use of the term Chaldean in Daniel is made in reference to the youths being carried to Babylon for training. They were chosen because they were the type of youths to **"whom they might teach the learning and the tongue of the Chaldeans."** (1:4) An initial reading of this would actually lead one to believe it refers to a different race or nation, in that they had their own language. The interpretation that this verse refers to a group of wise men or magicians is not explicit (or implicit) in the passage itself. This assumption must therefore be based upon other factors. I believe once more, that criticism here is founded in the preconceived assumption that the Book of Daniel was not written by Daniel the prophet.

The second example of the use of the term Chaldean is found in verse two of the second chapter of Daniel:

> **Then the king commanded to call the magicians, and the astrologers, and the sorcerers, and the Chaldeans, for to shew the king his dreams. So they came and stood before the king.**

First, I believe that this verse implies that the Chaldeans were *not* magicians, astrologers or sorcerers, but comprised a separate group. In fact, when examined closely, the book of Daniel consistently seems to indicate the Chaldeans were actually a distinct group. Also, the passage seems to indicate the Chaldeans were a group that would have been called to assist with this type of a problem, that they had some area of expertise that might be of value in solving it.

If you recall the writings of Herodotus regarding the Chaldeans, that they officiated in religious responsibilities in the temple. I suggest that the Chaldeans were not magicians, sorcerers or soothsayers, but administrators and priests. It not only makes sense, but should be considered a necessary component of the inquiries being made by the king. I find it unreasonable to assume that help from the gods would not be sought with such an important query.

Within this context, the passage would read "called the magicians, and the astrologers, and the sorcerers, and the priests, for to shew the king his dreams." Applying the role of priest to the Chaldeans here makes much more sense than asserting the term Chaldeans was used redundantly.

Note also, that Nebuchadnezzar and his father were both Chaldeans, in the racial sense. It is interesting to note that any direct dialogue between these groups and the king is always done with the Chaldeans, in other places besides this one. They appear to have held a position of leadership or administration, which also appears to correspond with the observations of Herodotus. I suggest that the Chaldeans may have been those who were the supervisors or leaders of the religious and administrative activities of the kingdom, and not simply magicians or astrologers. It must be stated clearly, however, that this is just the beginning of theory, but it would be an interesting topic for further research.

Issues from Criticism 2 – In Conclusion
1 – Did Daniel misuse the term "Chaldean?" No. In fact, Daniel appears to have use them in two different contexts. He makes reference to Chaldean's in their cultural perspective more than once. Daniel's mention to them, in reference to the function in Babylonian society, appears to correspond to the description give by Herodotus to the Chaldeans less than a century later.

Criticism #3: Daniel 2

The Issues:
1 - Did Daniel misidentify the fourth kingdom at the base of the statue from the King's dream?
2 – Was Daniel's dating of the dream in the second year of Nebuchadnezzar's reign an error?

We will now examine Chapter 2, which introduces the first dream of Nebuchadnezzar. It has been my goal, as much as is possible, to avoid interpretation or detailed commentary on the dreams, visions and prophecy of Daniel. However, the dream related in this chapter has become a significant part of the debate over the book's dating and accuracy, and I feel that some discussion is required.

The story in this chapter begins with Nebuchadnezzar and a dream which he received. He knew the dream was important, but was unable to remember it and had no idea as to its meaning. He quickly gathered his advisors and wise men and demanded they tell him what the dream was and what it meant. They were unable to do this, and Nebuchadnezzar became so angry that he ordered that the wise men were to be killed. Daniel finally found out about this problem when he was about to be put to death, and asked for a little time so that he could provide the king with the knowledge he required. Daniel then asked God for help, and was subsequently taken before the king, where he could relate and interpret the dream.

We can now examine the dream itself, which was the main focus of the chapter and the modern debate:

> **Thou, O king, sawest, and behold a great image. This great image, whose brightness was excellent,**

> stood before thee; and the form thereof was terrible. This image's head was of fine gold, his breast and his arms of silver, his belly and his thighs of brass, His legs of iron, his feet part of iron and part of clay. Thou sawest till that a stone was cut out without hands, which smote the image upon his feet that were of iron and clay, and brake them to pieces. (2:31-34)

According to Daniel's interpretation, the head of gold was Nebuchadnezzar himself (v. 38). His kingdom would be followed "**by another kingdom inferior to thee, and another third kingdom of brass, which shall bear rule over all the earth.**" (v. 39) The last kingdom will be "strong as iron" and will break and subdue "all things," (v. 40) and will be divided into other kingdoms represented by the toes of the statue. (v. 41) The statue will be destroyed by God's kingdom, represented by a stone which stuck the statue on its feet and destroyed it.

The controversy we will initially discuss revolves around the kingdoms which correspond to the four parts of the statue. The first is obviously the kingdom of Nebuchadnezzar, but how do we identify the three kingdoms which were to follow? The question was well defined by Donald E. Gowan in his book on Daniel:

> The prevailing reading through much of history assumed that the fourth kingdom must be Rome, the power of which would be well represented by iron, "which shall rule over the whole earth" (v. 39); and that is appropriate. This leaves Persia for the second kingdom, and to explain why it is called "inferior" to

Nebuchadnezzar's has required great ingenuity, for Persia was "inferior" in no respect.

The more natural reading, accepted by almost all commentators at present, is to take the second kingdom as the Medes ("inferior" inasmuch as it is of much less importance in Jewish history than Babylon); the third as the Persians, well described as ruling the whole earth; and the fourth, crushing and shattering everything as Alexander's. The division of his kingdom just after his death and the diplomatic marriages that affected Jewish history (2:42-43; 11:6) are then easily to be seen as represented by the mixture of iron and ceramic in the statue's feet. The Roman theory has found it necessary to struggle to find historical references in this symbolism, which fits the hellenistic period much more clearly.[27]

The traditional understanding of Daniel's interpretation, as stated, was that the progression of kingdoms was Neo-Babylonian (Nebuchadnezzar), Persian/Median, Greek (Alexander) and Roman. A common interpretation further identifies the ten toes as the kingdoms which developed after the break-up of the Roman Empire, and possibly the subsequent governments which exist today. As Daniel became the subject of critical scrutiny during the last few hundred years, it became apparent that Chapters 2 and 7 contained enough prophetic accuracy that it challenged the universal application of *vaticinia ex eventu*.

Even if it had been written in the middle of the second-century B.C., the Roman Empire was not a certain candidate to fill the description of the fourth kingdom, and that it would be broken into smaller kingdoms was clearly beyond the capabilities of a normal observer to predict. Sixth century or second century B.C., if Daniel predicted that the Roman Empire would be broken up into smaller kingdoms, it could not have been the result of normal deductive processes.

So, several centuries ago scholars were forced to reexamine Daniel. Once it became the accepted opinion that Daniel was historical rather than prophetic, these chapters also had to be reinterpreted. With a date of 168-165 a critical necessity, this meant that the fourth kingdom could not be Rome, since its establishment as an empire would not have occurred prior to this date. The obvious answer to this problem was to substitute Alexander and his empire for that of the Romans. Alexander had established his realm well before Daniel's accepted date of authorship and would therefore require no prophetic inspiration for its inclusion in the work.

This, however, caused another problem. There were four sections to the statue, but only three kingdoms (Babylonian, Persian and Greek) were commonly identified. The missing kingdom was quickly interpreted as Medea. This provided an adequate sequence for the stories from Daniel, one which fit within the accepted historical framework.

However, once this sequence was established, it became the source for further criticism. This criticism was not directed at those who had changed the traditional understanding of the kingdoms, and introduced this new and revised explanation for these revelations, but at the Book of Daniel itself. Allow me to quote from Pfeiffer's *Introduction to the Old Testament*:

> The series of four successive monarchies (chs. 2 and 7), of which the first is indubitably the Neo-Babylonian or Chaldean (625-538) and the fourth certainly the Hellenistic empire of

Alexander (and the kingdoms of his successors) requires the anachronistic displacement of the Medic and Persian (550-330). As a matter of fact the Medic kingdom (625-550) was conquered by Cyrus before the Neo-Babylonian[28]

I would like to quickly review the events which brought us to this new criticism of Daniel. For nearly two thousand years, almost every person reading and studying the book of Daniel believed that the legs and feet were the Roman Empire and subsequent kingdoms. With the resurgence of the critical approach to the interpretation of the book, Daniel was reclassified as a historical rather than prophetic text. This, then, required alternate explanations of some sections, including the interpretation of the dream in chapter two. The prophetic sections were then re-explained within their new historical contexts. Regarding chapter two, they were forced to create a new empire, and a Median empire was the only one which would fit.

It must be pointed out that many conservative scholars, supporting the traditional views of Daniel, cried, "Hey, that's not right. There was no Median Empire. You need to revise your interpretations back to include Rome." These complaints went largely ignored.

After the new interpretation had been accepted, it was then examined more closely by the liberal scholars. They noticed a problem and cried, "Hey, that's not right. There was no Median Empire. See, we told you there were errors."

This has not gone completely unnoticed, however. The problem this imposed interpretation causes has been recognized by a few of the critics themselves. Gowan writes:

> A stumbling block for complete

acceptance of the sequence - Babylon, Medes, Persia, Hellenistic kingdoms - has been the fact that there was no Median empire that intervened chronologically between the NeoBabylonian and the Persian kingdoms.29

It is somewhat paradoxical that critics have imposed this unwanted historical inaccuracy regarding the Medes, and then established it as an important part of their criticism of the book. The issue becomes even more perplexing because its obvious historical inaccuracy has in no way eroded the credence it is given. Most current studies of Daniel continue to portray Media as the second empire and then use this error to assault the accuracy of the book.

As stated above, the only reason for the problematic "displacement of the Medic and Persian" empires is the re-interpretation of the fourth kingdom as Greece instead of Rome. Since Roman history fits Daniel's description as well, and probably better, than Greece, the reason for the change is not due to history or to factors within the book of Daniel itself.

This, then, provides us with another example of the desired conclusion being the determining criteria for interpretation of the facts, instead of an objective examination of the facts being used to determine the conclusion. Almost everyone, conservative and liberal, agrees that the second empire in Daniel 2 cannot be accurately applied to the Medes. I believe that without the imperative of imposing an interpretation void of prophetic possibilities, the idea of a Median Empire would never have been suggested in the first place.

Another source of criticism in this chapter relates to it having occurred "**in the second year of the reign of Nebuchadnezzar**." (2:1) Chapter 1 of Daniel relates that his training took three years, so it would be impossible that Daniel would have completed his training and been one of the "Chaldeans" at this time. The suggestion is that the author is inconsistent in his dating of events.

However, a closer look at this chapter may offer us an alternative, possibly better explanation. In verse 2 we are given a list of those who were called before the king, "**Then the king commanded to call the magicians, and the astrologers, and the sorcerers, and the Chaldeans, for to shew the king his dreams**." The implication is that most, if not all, the wise men were called.

A few verses later we find out that Daniel is not even aware of what is happening. "**He [Daniel] answered and said to Arioch the king's captain, Why is the decree so hasty from the king? Then Arioch made the thing known to Daniel. Then Daniel went in, and desired of the king that he would give him time, and that he would shew the king the interpretation.**" (15, 16)

If Daniel had already finished his training and been one of the wise men, he would have probably been called before the king at first. Certainly, he would at least be aware of what was happening. If, however, he was still being trained by the Chaldeans, then one would expect these events to come as a surprise to him. The story in chapter two, after careful examination, may actually make more sense as written. Also, the criticism suggested does not appear as compelling when examined within this context.

I wish to make one other point regarding this question. If the scenario suggested above is correct, and Daniel interpreted the kings dream while still a student, an incident in chapter one may be easier to understand. Verses seventeen through twenty of chapter one state:

> **As for these four children, God gave them knowledge and skill in all learning and wisdom: and Daniel had understanding in all visions and**

> dreams. Now at the end of the days that the king had said he should bring them in, then the prince of the eunuchs brought them in before Nebuchadnezzar. And the king communed with them; and among them all was found none like Daniel, Hananiah, Mishael, and Azariah: therefore stood they before the king. And in all matters of wisdom and understanding, that the king enquired of them, he found them ten times better than all the magicians and astrologers that were in all his realm.

If, as students, they had been able to demonstrate their "understanding in all visions and dreams," then their enthusiastic reception by the king now makes more sense. They had already demonstrated this ability, and created a powerful impression on the king, because of the incident recorded in the second chapter which had previously occurred during their training.

Issued from Criticism 3:
1 - Did Daniel misidentify the fourth kingdom at the base of the statue from the King's dream? No. In fact, the interpretation of Daniel's defenders has remained constant, while the assertions of the book's critics have been forced to change as our knowledge expands.
2 – Was Daniel's dating of the dream in the second year of Nebuchadnezzar's reign an error? I don't believe so. It is very consistent with the book itself to assert that the dream occurred while they were still students, before their graduation in the third year.

Criticism #4: Daniel 4:30-33

The Issues:
1 – Did Nebuchadnezzar go through seven years of madness?
2 – Does these verses really refer to Nabonidus?

The Verse in Question:

> 4:30-33 The king spake, and said, is not this great Babylon, that I have built for the house of the kingdom by the might of my power, and for the honor of my majesty? While the word was in the king's mouth, there fell a voice from heaven, saying, O king Nebuchadnezzar, to thee it is spoken; The kingdom is departed from thee. And they shall drive thee from men, and thy dwelling shall be with the beasts of the field: they shall make thee to eat grass as oxen, and seven times shall pass over thee, until thou know that the most High ruleth in the kingdom of men, and giveth it to whomsoever he will. The same hour was the thing fulfilled upon Nebuchadnezzar: and he was driven from men, and did eat grass as oxen, and his body was wet with the dew of heaven, till his hairs were grown like eagles' feathers, and his nails like birds' claws.

The traditional interpretation of this event states that Nebuchadnezzar was cursed with a period of madness. Because of his pride and self-glorification, his senses were stripped from him, and he became like a beast of the fields. This condition lasted for a period usually believed to be seven years, until he recognized the power of God and was healed.

If this story is accurate, the king of Babylon would have experienced an extended period of illness and incapacitation. Critics, therefore, have a problem with this passage for several reasons. First, if he had been reduced to a life more animal than human, why was he not assassinated or replaced? Second, there is no independent mention of a period of madness in Nebuchadnezzar's life. Third, they contend that the reference to Nebuchadnezzar's madness was a mistake, and the reference should have been to Nabonidus instead.

First, there are several reasons why Nebuchadnezzar would not have been replaced during this period. This event occurred near the end of his life, and a successor had already been designated. Amal-Marduk would have assumed the duties of king in the event of death or incapacity of his father, and nothing would have been gained by Nebuchadnezzar's enemies if they had succeeded in removing him. Furthermore, Nebuchadnezzar had created an efficient and well organized bureaucracy, and it would certainly have continued to function without him.

We also need to understand that Nebuchadnezzar would not have been considered mad. His condition would probably have been attributed to an act of the gods, who would have taken control of the king or been in communion with him. This could have been seen as a sign of favor with the gods more than a disability.

There is also a question as to how long this condition lasted. The account does not state it continued for seven years, but this is the common interpretation. The passage could also be interpreted as seven seasons, or seven periods. It is possible that instead of seven years it actually did continue for seven seasons, or possibly only seven months, both long enough periods for the description of Nebuchadnezzar's condition to be achieved. Also, the fact that the number seven was used may signify that the number is a symbolic reference rather than a specific chronological reference. The specific length is not as important as the lesson it taught.

The next criticism deals with the fact that there is no extra-Biblical mention of Nebuchadnezzar's madness. On its own this cannot be considered proof that it did not happen, and is only suggested by critics because it compliments the other perceived problems with this story. While our knowledge is expanding, we still know very little about what went on throughout much of Nebuchadnezzar's reign. There is a long period near the end of his life when the only event recorded is the capture of Tyre. The lack of historical confirmation is certainly not conclusive, because the events of chapter four could easily have occurred during this time when almost nothing, on any subject, is known.

There are actually some question as to whether this event was recorded outside of the Bible. A reference from the Greek historian Abydenus is mentioned by Eusebius.[30] The reference says Nebuchadnezzar, near the end of his life, was possessed by a god, and a reference is made to information being given him by the Chaldeans. There are enough similarities here to suggest that there is historical evidence to confirm this event.

At this point, I would like to point out a problem with the defenders of Daniel. Many supporters of an early date have suggested that there is no mention of his madness because no one would want to publicize the fact that their king had gone mad. Leon Wood writes:

> Asserting that ancient writers make
> no mention of this sickness in regard to

Nebuchadnezzar, liberal expositors hold that the record cannot be historical. To this it may be replied, for one thing, that such an omission in official records is only to be expected. Kings wrote of matters pleasant to them, not of the unpleasant.[31]

Wood's book on Daniel is, overall, an excellent work, which I very much enjoyed. I find this an isolated example of misplaced apologetics.

I feel the argument that they would hide the King's condition from the world to be baseless, and shows a lack of consistency. Those asserting that the court would be ashamed and conceal his madness, also frequently make the argument that the madness would be seen as a blessing from the gods. There is an obvious lack of consistency between these two positions – if the madness was seen as a sign from the gods, it would not have been an embarrassment and hidden, if it was hidden it was probably not considered a sign from the gods.

Worse, it displays a lack of attention to the scripture itself. This chapter is presented as a letter from Nebuchadnezzar himself and begins:

> **Nebuchadnezzar the king, unto all people, nations, and languages, that dwell in all the earth; Peace be multiplied unto you. I thought it good to shew the signs and wonders that the high God hath wrought toward me. How great are his signs! and how mighty are his wonders! His kingdom is an everlasting kingdom, and his dominion is from generation to generation. (4: 1-3)**

The scripture itself stands in direct contradiction

to those who believe it's omission from historical reference was due to shame or an intentional effort to conceal it. The book of Daniel states that the king is very proud of the experience and personally published it to the world. It should be noted that this reference does support the argument that his madness was seen as a sign from God, or the gods, depending on perspective.

This misinterpretation by Daniel's supporters does not affect the veracity of the account. Its perceived lack of mention in historical records does not prove, or even substantially suggest, that the event never occurred.

The final criticism of this chapter asserts that this account is really a reference to Nabonidus and not to Nebuchadnezzar; the fact that it is attributed to Nebuchadnezzar is suggested as proof of its historical inaccuracy. This argument is based on one of the Dead Sea Scrolls (4QOrNab), the *Prayer of Nabonidus*.

This criticism also appears to be an attempt to fit the facts to the desired conclusion. As we examine the differences and similarities between the stories in Daniel and the Prayer of Nabonidus, we will find that their similarities are not as great as their differences:

- The affliction of Nabonidus lasted seven years, and Nebuchadnezzar's lasted seven periods of time.
- Nabonidus wrote about the incident, as Nebuchadnezzar did with the letter in Ch. 2.
- Nabonidus has an ulcer, a severe skin disease and was not affected mentally. Nebuchadnezzar's was mental.
- Nabonidus has complete control of his faculties and prays unsuccessfully to his pagan gods during this time. Nebuchadnezzar was not lucid enough to do this.
- The incident of Nabonidus' affliction occurs

at Tema and not Babylon.
- No mention is made in the Qumran text of Nabonidus acting or appearing like an animal.
- Nabonidus is cured by a Jewish exorcist and not by God.

There are undeniable similarities, which I will readily acknowledge. I find it interesting, however, that with the number of texts with the book of Daniel, found in every cave at Qumran, as opposed to this one fragment of the Prayer of Nabonidus, that the assumption was not made that the Prayer was inspired by Daniel instead of the opposite being true? I find the suggestion that Daniel was the source instead of the copy to be much more likely – if indeed they both refer to the same event.

Issues from Criticism 4:
1 – Did Nebuchadnezzar go through seven years of madness? This is a trick question. While there is no way to disprove this reference, and actual historical evidence that it may well have occurred, the book doesn't definitively claim it was for seven years.
2 – Do these verses really refer to Nabonidus? Unlikely. It is difficult to elevate a few scraps of story, found in a single cave, over the enormous volume of evidence for Daniel itself. Examples of Daniel occur in almost every location where ancient documents are found.

CRITICISM #5: Daniel 5:1-7

The Issues:
1 – Does the reference to Nebuchadnezzar as the father of Belshazzar show a lack of knowledge of Babylonian History?
2 - Was Belshazzar really the King of

Babylon?

The Verse in Question:

> Daniel 5:1-7 Belshazzar the king made a great feast to a thousand of his lords, and drank wine before the thousand. Belshazzar, whiles he tasted the wine, commanded to bring the golden and silver vessels which his father Nebuchadnezzar had taken out of the temple which was in Jerusalem; that the king, and his princes, his wives, and his concubines, might drink therein. Then they brought the golden vessels that were taken out of the temple of the house of God which was at Jerusalem; and the king, and his princes, his wives, and his concubines, drank in them. They drank wine, and praised the gods of gold, and of silver, of brass, of iron, of wood, and of stone. In the same hour came forth fingers of a man's hand, and wrote over against the candlestick upon the plaster of the wall of the king's palace: and the king saw the part of the hand that wrote. Then the king's countenance was changed, and his thoughts troubled him, so that the joints of his loins were loosed, and his knees smote one against another. The king cried aloud to bring in the astrologers, the Chaldeans, and the soothsayers. And the king spake, and said to the wise men of Babylon, Whosoever shall read this writing,

> **and shew me the interpretation thereof, shall be clothed with scarlet, and have a chain of gold about his neck, and shall be the third ruler in the kingdom.**

The question discussed in this section centers around Belshazzar, and two statements regarding him. The first problem is that he claims Nebuchadnezzar is his father, when we know his father was Nabonidus. The second problem is that these verses assert that Belshazzar was, or was at least referred to, as "king." According to king lists and other historical sources, it was Nabonidus who ruled that Babylonian empire at this time.

Let's examine these problems, beginning with the question of Belshazzar's parentage. Why does Daniel refer to Belshazzar as Nebuchadnezzar's father? Farrell Till makes a detailed presentation of the critical view below:

> If Daniel achieved such prominence in Nebuchadnezzar's kingdom, he would have surely been familiar with the king's family, but in chapter five, the writer of this story referred to Nebuchadnezzar five times as the "father" of Belshazzar. One of these references was made by the writer himself in the narration of the story, two of the references were attributed to the queen, one of them to Belshazzar himself, and the fifth to Daniel as he addressed the king. In this address to the king, Daniel also referred to Belshazzar as Nebuchadnezzar's "son," so in less than one chapter, six incorrect references were made to Belshazzar's relationship to Nebuchadnezzar.[32]

There is no disputing the fact that Belshazzar was not actually the son of Nebuchadnezzar, but of Nabonidus the current king. Having established this, we still need to examine whether there is any justification for the relationship between Belshazzar and Nebuchadnezzar being referred to in this way.

So, is there any valid reason why Nebuchadnezzar would be called the father of Belshazzar? Actually, there are several. It was not uncommon for a ruler or king to claim to be a descendant from a famous monarch from the past. Even if not from the same royal lineage, the fact that a person later sat on the same throne was, at times, taken as justification for kinship. Here is an example:

> A rebel against Darius I was described in the Behistun inscription: "One man, Phraortes by name, a Median - he rose up in Media. To the people thus he said, 'I am Khshartrita, of the family of Cyaxares.'" It is assumed that this pretender was calling upon the glory of his distant ancestor, Khshathrita, father of Cyaxares (Phraortes), just as other rebels against Darius claimed to be Nebuchadnezzar redivivi.[33]

This quote provides us with examples of those attempting to seize power, and attempting to justify and validate their claims by asserting a relationship with past kings. It gives us only two of the many examples of this occurring.

There are also more straight-forward explanations for the reference to Nebuchadnezzar being Belshazzar's father. One important clarification involves the word "father" itself. The Semitic languages used the word father to refer to male ancestors. In the

Hebrew and Aramaic languages of that time, the term for grandfather, or great-grandfather, did not exist. In referring to one's grandfather it would be necessary to say 'my fathers' father', but in these and other contexts, the term father would simply be used. The same reasoning would apply to the term son meaning actual son or grandson.

Daniel himself provides us with an example of this. In chapter eleven we have the following quote:

> **He shall enter peaceably even upon the fattest places of the province; and he shall do that which his fathers have not done, nor his fathers' fathers; he shall scatter among them the prey, and spoil, and riches: yea, and he shall forecast his devices against the strong holds, even for a time.** (v. 24)

Even though it could be argued that no actual relationship is required in order to refer to a male predecessor as father, it will still be worthwhile to determine if Belshazzar was, in fact, justified in calling Nebuchadnezzar his 'father' based on an actual family relationship. One interesting possibility is that Nabonidus' mother, Belshazzar's grandmother, may have considered herself a daughter to Nebuchadnezzar. We read from a stele discovered in Harran written by Belshazzar's grandmother:

> I have made Nabonidus, the son whom I bore, serve Nebuchadnezzar, son of Nabopolassar, and Neriglissar, king of Babylon, and he performed his duty for them day and night by doing always what was their pleasure. He also made me a

good name before them and they gave me an elevated position as if I were their real daughter.[34]

With the blessing of Nebuchadnezzar himself, Belshazzar's grandmother may have considered herself a daughter of the former king. We know that the statement regarding Nabonidus being in the service of Nebuchadnezzar is true, it is confirmed by the fact that he was sent by the king to negotiate a treaty between the Lydians and the Medes. Nabonidus was a favorite in the courts of Nebuchadnezzar, and his mother claims she was considered a daughter to the king. This, by itself, would be enough to justify, in Belshazzar's mind, the claim to being the son of Nebuchadnezzar.

However, this explanation would surely be unacceptable to critics of an early date of authorship, and fortunately is not the only link between Nebuchadnezzar and Belshazzar. Regarding Nabonidus ascension to the throne, we are told:

> After his death, Neriglissar was succeeded by his son Labashi-Marduk who was still a child but, we are told, exhibited such signs of wickedness that his friends plotted and, nine months later, tortured him to death. The conspirators then met and decided to raise to the throne one of them, Nabu-na'id (Nabonidus), (June 556 B.C.) . . . A man in his sixties when he ascended the throne, he had held important administrative functions under Nebuchadrezzar and Neriglissar.[35]

Even though Nabonidus was from the nobility, but he would still be considered a "usurper, not related to Nebuchadnezzar"[36] and therefore had no legitimate claim to the throne. One way to strengthen his claim to legitimacy would be to marry into the royal family, and this is what happened. Nabonidus was married to Nebuchadnezzar's daughter Nitocris, possibly for this reason.

To better understand the relationship between Nabonidus, Belshazzar and Nebuchadnezzar, we will refer to the genealogical royal descent lines compiled by David Hughes. Mr. Hughes is experienced in genealogical research and has focused much of his research into the royal genealogy of this period. His compilation and comprehensive study of available sources clearly illustrates that Belshazzar was a descendent of Nebuchadnezzar. Belshazzar was the son of "Nabonidus, Babylonian Emperor 556-539, & Neitaqert (Nitocris), daughter of NEBUCHADNEZZAR II "THE GREAT" of Babylonia & 3rd wife, Neitaqert (Nitokris)"[37]

Belshazzar was actually Nebuchadnezzar's grandson, through his mother Nitocris. Even Driver, a well-known and outstanding critic of Daniel was forced to admit this possibility:

> As regards Belshazzar's relationship to Nebuchadnezzar, there remains the *possibility* that Nabu-nahid may have sought to strengthen his position by marrying a daughter of Nebuchadnezzar, in which case the latter might be spoken of as Belshazzar's father (=grandfather, by Hebrew usage).[38]

It is very difficult, at this point, for the critics to justify using Daniel's references to Belshazzar referring to Nebuchadnezzar as his father, as proof of poor historical knowledge. On this point, Daniel has consistently been shown to be correct.

Against this argument, there are some who attempt to assert that Belshazzar could not have been born of the union of Nitocris and Nabonidus. To answer this, we need only refer to the words of Herodotus. In the first book of his history he identifies all three of these people. Nabonidus is referred to as Labynetus, who negotiated the treaty between the Medes and Lydians (1.74.1) and was king at the time of Croesus fall to Cyrus (1.77.1). There can be no question that this is Nabonidus. The references to Nitocris are also interesting, because it seems there was more written about her activities than to those of her husband. "The later of the two queens [of Babylon], whose name was Nitocris, a wiser princess than her predecessor" (1.185.1). Herodotus then goes on to talk about the son of Nitocris. "The expedition of Cyrus was undertaken against the son of this princess [Nitocris], who bore the same name as his father Labynetus, and was king of the Assyrians." (1.188.1) The son of Nitocris, ruling in Babylon at the time of Cyrus's conquest of Babylon, could be none other than Belshazzar.

I would like to leave this topic with one additional comment. As Till pointed out above, the number of references to the relationship of Belshazzar to Nebuchadnezzar does seem unusual. One may get the impression that Belshazzar wanted to emphasize that his claim to the throne went back to Nebuchadnezzar, and not simply to Nabonidus. Belshazzar was in Babylon while his father was living in the Arabian dessert, because Nabonidus had been rejected by the religious and commercial establishments of Babylon. Nabonidus was probably considered to be somewhat bizarre, and it is quite understandable that Belshazzar may want everyone to understand that his authority went back to the great king Nebuchadnezzar, and didn't rest solely on the authority of his father.

The second part of the discussion of this passage deals with Daniel's reference to Belshazzar as king. Driver writes, "Belshazzar is represented as *king* of Babylon . . . In point of fact, Nabonidus (Nabu-nahid) was the last king of Babylon . . The inscriptions thus lend no support to the hypothesis."[39]

Nabonidus left the city of Babylon for ten years.

During that time his own accounts record limited contact with events in the capital city. Having essentially abandoned the city of Babylon, he "had left the government in the hands of his son Bel-shar-usar ('Belshazzar' of the Old Testament)."[40] Belshazzar ruled in the capital city of the Empire effectively unsupervised, the term "king" is quite appropriate, and would probably have been required by Belshazzar.

In fact, there was a long-standing tradition that contradicts the idea that Belshazzar could not act in the duties of the king. Even before the Neo-Babylonian period, the training of the crown prince, in this case Belshazzar, was important. In this training "he was prepared for his royal functions and gradually entrusted with important administrative duties, which included replacing the king as head of the state in time of war."[41] The time of Nabonidus' stay in Arabia was due in part to his war against the Arab tribes.

This point has been effectively conceded by some critics. Almost all true scholars echo the sentiment of Philip R. Davies:

> But it has been clear since 1924 that although Nabonidus was the last king of the neo-Babylonian dynasty, Belshazzar was effectively ruling Babylon. In this respect, then, Daniels is correct. The literal meaning of 'son' should not be pressed; even if it might betray a misunderstanding on the part of Daniel.[42]

In the early 19th century, this was one of the certain and unquestionable proofs of Daniel's historical inaccuracies. Aside from Daniel, there were no existent references, from any other source, to Belshazzar at this the time. It appears that the name of Belshazzar vanished completely in the 5th century B.C., not to reappear.

What was once a fatal flaw in the scripture is now

a clear indication that Daniel had knowledge that appears to have been unavailable at the late date of authorship. A Jewish scholar, writing in the second-century B.C., could not have know about Belshazzar. Daniel, a member of the court during his sixth-century B.C., would have known. Strong evidence that Daniel was indeed the author.

The Issues from Criticism #5:
1 – Does the reference to Nebuchadnezzar as the father of Belshazzar show a lack of knowledge of Babylonian History? No, in fact it may demonstrate a very strong understanding of that period of Babylonian history. This claim by Belshazzar would be acceptable based only on historical precedence. Many rulers claimed dependency from great figures from the past, whether genealogically accurate or not. More importantly, this verse may demonstrate an extraordinarily accurate understanding of this period. It appears that Belshazzar was the son of Nitocris, daughter of Nebuchadnezzar, This would make Belshazzar Nebuchadnezzar's grandson, and that relationship would have been referred to as "father and son."

2 - Was Belshazzar really the King of Babylon? Yes. This is a strong element in support of Biblical accuracy. The name Belshazzar was lost to history for thousands of years. If Daniel had been written in the second-century B.C., the author would have had no knowledge of Belshazzar or his role in history. This is not an error, but a very strong evidence of an early date of authorship.

CRITICISM #6: Daniel 5:30,31 & 9:1

The Issues:
1 – Who was Darius the Mede, was he a real person?

5:30, 31 In that night was Belshazzar the king of the Chaldeans slain. And Darius the Medean took the kingdom, being about threescore and two years old.

The Verse in Question:

> **9:1 In the first year of Darius the son of Ahasuerus, of the seed of the Medes, which was made king over the realm of the Chaldeans;**

We will deal with the verses in these two sections together because they introduce the same questions: Was Darius the Mede a real person? If so, who was he? It is universally accepted that it was the armies of Cyrus, king of the growing Persian Empire, which conquered Babylon, and it is Cyrus who follows Nabonidus on official king's lists.

This fact is not in dispute, but it does not answer the questions at hand. There are numerous examples of the king of an empire placing, or allowing other kings to rule over their local nations. This is illustrated by the kings of Judah who, continued for a time under Pharaoh and Nebuchadnezzar. The bible refers to the rulers on Jerusalem as king, but the true kings reigned in either Egypt or Babylon. Cyrus was King of Persia, but that does not preclude another assuming kingship in Babylon. Belshazzar does not appear on the king's list either, though we have already established his kingship.

We herein deal with the several statements which describe Darius. First, he captured Babylon; second, he was a Mede; third, he was about sixty-two years old; fourth, his father was named Ahasuerus; fifth, he was made king over Babylon.

Before we begin to discuss these individual statements identifying Darius the Mede, we should probably get an overview of the topic as a whole. The possible candidates are Cyrus himself, being referred to by the name of Darius. Also, there are two men by the name of Gubaru - Gubaru I (Gobryas, Ugbaru) and Gubaru II (Gobryas II). The first was the general who captured the city for Cyrus, and the second an administrator who later ruled the land of Babylon for Cyrus. Others have been suggested, such as Cambyses (Cyrus' son who ruled Babylon) and Astyages (former Medean king and Cyrus' grandfather), but these are very unlikely and do not bear close scrutiny.

Let us, then, examine this initial list of characteristics of Darius. First, he captured Babylon. We have two candidates for this accomplishment, Cyrus, King of the Persians and Gubaru I/Gobryas who was the general who actually captured Babylon for Cyrus. The Babylonian Chronicles confirm that Gubaru I was the person who first occupied the city.[43] The requirement for Darius stating that he "took the kingdom" applies equally well to both of them. There is no existing evidence which indicates Gubaru II participated in the capture of Babylon.

Second, Darius was a Mede. At first glance this creates a problem for Cyrus, who was obviously Persian. But it must be remembered that Cyrus is commonly recognized as the grandson of Astyages, the Median King. Astyages gave his daughter, Mandane, to the Persian King Cambyses as wife; Cyrus was their son. One source that verifies this is the ancient Greek historian Xenophon, who wrote in his history "At that time Astyages sent for his daughter and her son; for he was desirous to see him, having heard that he was a handsome and excellent child. Accordingly Mandane went to her father, and took her son Cyrus with her."

The Greeks and Hebrews both continued referring to the Persians as Medes long after the Medean Empire was absorbed into the Persian. There can be no question that a reference to Cyrus as a Mede has ample justification and precedence from a historical perspective.

It is difficult to establish with absolute certainty whether Gubaru I can be called a 'Mede'. He was from one of the northern Babylonian provinces, and was actually the governor of the province of Gutium under Nabonidus. Babylon had gained control over much of the land to its north because when "Cyrus of Persia rebelled against the Medes, Nabonidus used the occasion to seize the Median-held city of Harran where his aged mother was a priestess of the moon."[44]

Several commentaries suggest that Gutium was, at the time of the Persian invasion, part of the Babylonian empire. If Gutium also was land annexed by Nabonidus when the Medean Empire began to collapse, the possibility of the local governor being a Mede, governing a formerly Median province, remains entirely possible. It is also interesting that these commentaries state that when given the opportunity, Gubaru defected to the side of Cyrus without a fight and became the general of his army. These events would make sense if Gubaru were a Mede.

Gubaru II, governor of Babylon, has been associated with the family of Astyages, the last purely Median king. "The extent of a Median Empire before its absorption by the Persians under Cyrus is not clear. Thereafter the Medes were to play a subordinate though important role under the Persians in the Achaemenid period (550-330 B.C.)."[45] The Medes are often believed to have held important positions, including governors and generals, in the new Persian Empire.

In fact, there are some who propose that with Cyrus, the Medes had been 'unified' with the Persians as opposed to being conquered by them. Cyrus assumed rule without a war, because the Median forces simply surrendered and joined the Persians. "By uniting these two Iranian states he [Cyrus] laid the foundation of modern Iran. The fall of the Median Empire and this new confederacy of the Iranians under one strong ruler filled the neighbouring kings of Lydia and Babylon with alarm."[46]

The Median civilization was older, and in many ways dominated the emerging Persian culture. "The Achaemenids [Persians] were for some time tributaries to the Medians, who were superior to them in civilization."[47] The Medes had experience in managing an Empire, and Cyrus may well have taken advantage of that expertise. This leads to the possibility that a trusted relative from Ecbatana, Gubaru II, may well have been Cyrus' choice as governor of Babylon.

Third, he was about sixty-two years old. There is no consensus on the date of Cyrus's birth, though most sources place it around 600-590 B.C. The early date would make his age very close to that reported by Daniel. Some assign his birth to 601 B.C., but these are not reliable as they apparently calculate that date based on the assumption that he was Darius the Mede.

Regarding Gubaru I/Gobryas, according to the ancient Babylonian sources soon after Babylon was conquered, "In the month of Arahshamnu, on the night of the 11th day, Gobryas died." [48] This raises the likelihood that he was somewhat advanced in age, so he cannot be disqualified as a candidate based on age. It is also interesting to note that Daniel's references to Darius's rule in Babylon may have lasted only about a year, as references in 9:1 and 11:1. Daniel mentions events "in the first year" but no later.

There is no truly reliable information regarding the age of Gubaru II. If he were an uncle or cousin from the Medean royal family, an age near Cyrus' is certainly a possibility.

Daniel's reference to the age of sixty-two does not point conclusively to any of these people. While there is no definitive evidence pointing to one of the candidates, there is also every indication that all could have been that age at the time of Babylon's fall.

Another point of interest concerns the phrase used by Daniel to give the age of Darius, "**threescore and two**" years. This manner of expressing the number sixty-two is used again by Daniel relating to the time of the Messiah (9:25, 26). It is possible that there is a symbolic connotation to this number that we no longer understand, and that it may not refer to actual chronological age.

Fourth, we know that Cyrus' father was named Ahasuerus. Critics such as S.R. Driver, place a great deal of emphasis on this detail regarding Darius:

> Darius, son of Ahasuerus - elsewhere the Hebrew for of Xerxes, a *Mede,* after the defeat of Belshazzar, is "made king over the realm of the Chaldaeans" (5:31, 6:1, 9:1, 11:1). There seems to be no room for such a ruler. According to all other authorities, Cyrus is the immediate successor of Nabu-nahid, and the ruler of the entire Persian Empire. It has been conjectured that Darius may have been an under-king--perhaps either identical with the Cyaxares II of Xenophon, or a younger brother of Astyages--whom Cyrus may have made governor of Babylon.[49]

Driver is not the only one who assumes that the name "Ahasuerus" refers to Xerxes (485-465).[50] While it is very likely that the Hebrew name Ahasuerus did refer to Xerxes, it must be remembered that Xerxes was only a throne name. The name Ahasuerus could also have been used as a reference to other kings, or even kings in general.

The insistence that "Ahasuerus" refers to "Xerxes" may simply be an example of stopping when you find the answer you're looking for. Since Darius was an imaginary figure, how could his father be real? The assumption of skeptical investigators would be met. This would be precisely the type of error that would neatly fit a second-century B.C. author, confused about the intricacies of sixth-century B.C. history. Therefore, no further investigation was needed.

However, by continuing to explore other possibilities, an alternative answer does begin to appear. It is based on a characteristic of the old Semitic languages that we have previously discussed, that fact that there is no specific word for grandfather; that the term father is used for both.

Let's take a moment here and examine Cyrus' ancestry in light of this linguistic feature. If we assume that Astyages was Cyrus's grandfather, then his great-grandfather would have been Cyaxares. Since Cyaxares would have been called Cyrus "father," the Hebrew spelling of Cyaxares may well have been translated as "Ahasuerus," and could possibly be considered in reference to the statement "Darius, son of . . ." which could accurately be used to refer to his father, grandfather, great-grandfather, and on back.

William Shea makes the following argument:

> The individual whose name provides the best phonetic potential here is Cyaxares (Cyaxerxes). His name is attested in five languages: Old Persian, Elamite, Babylonian, Hebrew and Greek. . . While the correspondence is not perfect in any of the languages, there are enough resemblances so that the words can be recognizes as related to one another, allowing for individual scribal differences in the treatment of the original phonemes. At least there are enough correspondences here to propose that his is the name of the ancestor whose name lies behind Ahasuerus in Dan 9:1.[51]

The identification of Ahasuerus with Cyaxares is also suggested by the *Interpreters Commentary*. This commentary firmly supports the second-century date of authorship, but it states that the author of Daniel was probably familiar with Cyaxares as Ahasuerus because:

> by this Hebrew name the Median king know through Greek transcription as Cyaxares (ca. 625-ca. 585), who conquered Nineveh and largely created the Median Empire. Cyaxares' son was Astyages, who was ruler of this empire when it fell to Cyrus the Persian. Perhaps confused traditions linking the later Ahasuerus (Xerxes) to Darius the Great came to be mistakenly associated also with the earlier Ahasuerus (Cyaxares) and resulted in the misnaming of his son.[52]

There is significant support for the identification of Cyrus great-grandfather, Cyaxares, as the Ahasuerus mentioned here in Daniel. Let's go further with an explanation of why any references to him as Cyrus "father" can be considered accurate and appropriate. Let's consider why Daniel makes such an effort to demonstrate Cyrus' Median ancestry at all?

I suggest that it could have been an intentional effort to demonstrate the fulfillment of prophecy. The reference to Cyrus Median ancestry would show the fulfillment of prophecies by both Jeremiah and Isaiah. Jer 51:11 says: **Make bright the arrows; gather the shields: the LORD hath raised up the spirit of the kings of the Medes: for his device is against Babylon, to destroy it; because it is the vengeance of the LORD, the vengeance of his temple.** Cyrus was king of the Medes, and his capture of Babylon would confirm the words of these prophets. There may have been other reasons for Daniel's desire to emphasize the kingship over the Medes, but this alone would justify it.

Fifth, he was "made king over Babylon." There are

two possible ways to interpret that statement. It could simply mean that Darius 'became' king, in which case it would seem to refer to Cyrus, or that someone else was 'granted' the kingship, in which case either Gubaru I or II may qualify as candidates.

It was not uncommon for a local governor to be considered to hold the position of king of his region, while still governing by the dispensation of the king of the entire empire. We have addressed this to some extend with Belshazzar. In a similar fashion, the *Babylonian Chronicles* record that "Cyrus sent greetings to all Babylon. Gobryas [Gubaru], his governor installed (sub) governors in Babylon."[53] Contemporary sources confirm that Gobryas was indeed governor of Babylon. There are numerous examples of the title of "King" being applied to these governors, as in the previously mentioned kings of Judah.

Only two of the individuals discussed above adequately fill all of the requirements for consideration as Darius the Mede. There is no indication that Gubaru II was involved with the actual capture of Babylon, which leaves Gubaru I and Cyrus as the only possibilities. I will briefly discuss the arguments for and against each of them.

Gubaru precisely satisfies many of the characteristics of Darius. He conquered the city of Babylon, and Cyrus himself didn't enter the city until later.[54] In fact, Cyrus did not even claim the title of "King of Babylon" until later:

> Cyrus was known by various titles, which have been preserved in a number of ancient texts. . . In 90 percent of the four hundred cases checked, the standard royal titulary in economic texts for Cyrus was "King of Babylon, King of Lands." . . . Cyrus was called "King of Lands" at the beginning of his first year (538) and "King

of Babylon, King of Lands" at the end of his first year. He[55] concludes that the reason Cyrus did not carry the title "King of Babylon" during his first nine months was because Gubaru, the conqueror of Babylon, bore this title. He furthermore suggests that the later be identified as the enigmatic "Darius the Mede" of the Book of Daniel.[56]

One of the actions of Darius the Mede was to organize a government loyal to the new rulers. Daniel records "**It pleased Darius to set over the kingdom an hundred and twenty princes, which should be over the whole kingdom; And over these three presidents; of whom Daniel was first**." (6: 1, 2) As noted above, ancient texts from the period state that it was Gobryas [Gubaru] who began to install the administration of Babylon and chose these governors.

At this point in our presentation, we should point out that some scholars raise a serious question regarding the possibility of Gubaru I being identified with Darius. The Chronicle of Nabonidus states that "In the month of Arashamnu, on the night of the eleventh *[November 6]*, Gobryas died." Since his army had entered Babylon on the 13th of October, this means that Gubaru I ruled in Babylon for less than a month. This does create a serious time problem if we are going to assert that Gubaru I was Darius.

If Gubaru I indeed died less than a month after the conquest of Babylon, then this does not seem to be sufficient time for the organization of a government. Also, it must be remembered that the incident of Daniel and the lions occurred during the administration of Darius. This creates even more problems with Gubaru I satisfying the characteristics of Darius.

As short as this time is, there is a possible explanation, one which would also explain why Cyrus would relinquish command of his armies to a general who only days before had been an enemy. Cyrus had begun laying the groundwork for his conquest of the Babylonian Empire long before he began the actual military campaign. He had for years been courting the priests of Marduk, who were angry with Nabonidus. Professor Africa notes, "But while Nabonidus remained in Teima, Cyrus of Persia had set out to conquer the Near East, and his agents conspired with the discontented priests at Babylon."[57] It seems likely that he may also have contacted others to lay the groundwork for the military actions as well.

It is important to remember that this is similar to the way Cyrus defeated the Median Empire. While the exact details are unclear, all accounts agree that Cyrus did not defeat Astyages, the King of the Medes, in battle. The Median General Harpagus, at a critical point, simply changed sides and began to fight with Cyrus' forces.

If Gubaru were actually a Mede governing in lands recently controlled by the Chaldeans, Cyrus would probably have contacted him long before hostilities began. Cyrus would want to determine his loyalty to Babylon, and if possible orchestrate his defection. This follows very closely the way he defeated the Medes. Given his success, it is very easy to see why he would attempt it again.

The plan to combine the Gutium and Median/Persian forces under Gubaru would have had many advantages. As a governor in the Babylonian Empire, Gubaru would have had access to the city of Babylon itself. The knowledge gained from his visits would have allowed him to formulate a plan of attack based on an intimate, personal knowledge of the city.

It has always seemed incredible to me that the conquest of such an immense, well structured and organized defensive position was accomplished so quickly. The idea of a hastily prepared plan, executed by a newly combined, organized and commanded army being able to capture what was probably the best defended city in the world in a single night, seems more far-fetched than any of the other stories in Daniel.

The account of the collapse of the Babylonian empire relates that the surrender of the city of Sippar was followed the very next day by the capture of Babylon. This indicates a very sophisticated plan of battle. The likelihood that the plan was very well prepared, and possibly supported from inside Babylon, seems highly probable if not necessary. With the size of the city of Babylon, it probably would have taken detailed preparation just to be able to make their way to the palace in the time required to catch them unprepared.

Let me offer a suggestion regarding Daniel's selection as one of the presidents of the princes. If Gubaru had, as an official of the Babylonian government from the northern province of Gutium, made frequent visits to Babylon, then a previous relationship with Daniel was possible. They would have certainly had the opportunity, and as subjects from dominated lands possible the reason, to communicate. If Gubaru had prepared a detailed plan for the conquest of Babylon – which again seems much more believable than that it was accomplished in one day with little planning or preparation – it is equally possible he had prepared detailed plans for establishing control over the city once taken. One explanation for the appointment of Daniel so quickly was that he was a part of the plan long before the actual conquest began.

This would also add an interesting dimension to the interchange between Daniel and Belshazzar on the evening of the city's fall. Daniel's reply to Belshazzar's offer of riches for the interpretation of the writing on the wall was: "**Let thy gifts be to thyself, and give thy rewards to another; yet I will read the writing unto the king, and make known to him the interpretation.**" (5:17) Daniel is almost saying, "Keep it yourself. There is nothing you can do for me now."

Is this more than speculation? No. In fact, I am not really proposing this as a serious explanation at all. I have found nothing that would support any of the assertions of a previous relationship between Daniel and Gubaru, but that was not my objective. I was merely interested in the possibility of other scenarios.

Following this further, let us examine another quote regarding Darius the Mede:

> Accordingly we read that "Darius the Mede" (5:31), and not Cyrus or his general Gubaru (Gobryas), conquered Babylon. To add to the confusion this imaginary Darius living before Cyrus (6:26; 10:1) is said to be "the son of Ahasuerus [Xerxes, 485-465], of the seed of the Medes" (9:1). In the author's muddled mind the conquests of Babylon by Cyrus (538) and by Darius I 521 were identified and Darius, after being turned into a Mede, was placed before Cyrus; unless of course "Darius" is merely a title of Gobryas.[58]

Critics of an early date have attempted to commandeer the intellectual 'high ground' in this debate. They assert that anyone who has taken the time to educate themselves could concur only with the accuracy of *their* interpretations. They imply that to disagree with them is to succumb to superstition and be a participant in "the author's muddled" understanding of these events. My supposition regarding Gubaru I, as detailed above, was presented to suggest that there is at least one, and certainly many more, possible scenarios that reconcile an early date of authorship. I maintain that there is not enough information to make any definite assertions, either for or against any of these theories.

The political world of that period in general, and

the maneuverings between the Babylonian and Persian empires in particular, were probably as complicated and dynamic at that point in history as between any competing cultures today. We should be very careful in using the limited information we have today to dogmatically assert the correctness of any one historical scenario.

The second candidate for Darius the Mede is Cyrus. We have touched briefly on several of the reasons why Cyrus may qualify as Darius. There can be no question as to whether the capture of Babylon can be attributed to Cyrus; it was his army and his plan. The fact that his mother was almost certainly the daughter of the Median king qualifies him fully for being of the "seed of the Medes." It fact, racially he was as much a Mede as a Persian. He was approximately the right age, and Cyaxares, as the grandfather of Cyrus, is a very strong possibility for Ahasuerus.

However, there are some problems. We will begin with one of the most important questions, found in Daniel 6:28, "**So this Daniel prospered in the reign of Darius, and in the reign of Cyrus the Persian**." The initial impression is that there were two kings, and two periods of time covered. The first being that of Darius, and the second being that of Cyrus. Before we can seriously consider any other arguments, we need to understand what Daniel meant here. If Daniel is saying they were different rulers, this would preclude any further discussion of Cyrus being identified with Darius.

Yamauchi introduces the argument this way: [the proposal] "offered by D. J. Wiseman, was that Daniel 6:28 be translated, 'Daniel prospered in the reign of Darius even the reign of Cyrus the Persian,' that is, taking the former name as a throne name."[59] This would change the meaning of this scripture to indicate that Darius and Cyrus were indeed the same person, with Darius possibly being his throne name.

This is not a unique situation in the Bible. The Hebrew word in question here is *waw*. Older translations of our Bible render this word as 'and', employed as a conjunction. Wiseman suggests, however, an alternate translation where the word *waw* is used in an explicative way, with the second part further clarifying the first. This would be translated then as "even" or "that is" instead of "and." This would change the translation to read "So this Daniel prospered in the reign of Darius, that is, in the reign of Cyrus the Persian." This completely changes the message of this important passage.

We must now ask, is there any justification for this change? A look back at biblical interpretation does provide a very good parallel. It relates to the identification of a biblical character named Pul. The original King James Version has 1Chronicles 5:26 thusly, "**And the God of Israel stirred up the spirit of Pul king of Assyria, and the spirit of Tilgathpilneser king of Assyria, and he carried them away**." It had always been assumed that Pul and Tilgathpilneser were different people. There was no known reference to the name Pul, so it was naturally assumed by most critics that he was not an actual historical figure.

However, as time passed and more information was gathered, the question received an answer. It was learned that Pul and Tilgathpilneser were actually the same person.[60] The NIV now renders this verse "**So the God of Israel stirred up the spirit of Pul king of Assyria (that is, Tiglath-Pileser king of Assyria), who took the Reubenites, the Gadites and the half-tribe of Manasseh into exile**." This situation is almost identical to the one we are examining in Daniel, and the change made in Chronicles sets an important precedent relating to our passage in Daniel. Using this example from Chronicles, Daniel would be interpreted as saying that Cyrus and Darius were the same person.

The suggestion has been made that this

translation practice may also apply to the very next verse in Daniel, which reads, "**In the first year of Belshazzar king of Babylon Daniel had a dream and visions of his head upon his bed**." (7:1) The most reasonable interpretation of this passage is that "visions of his head" are explaining what the dreams mentioned were and not trying to separate them, which is exactly what we suggest for the verse under examination.

Other examples exist. Again in the fourth chapter of Daniel we read "**I saw in the visions of my head upon my bed, and, behold, a watcher and an holy one came down from heaven**." Daniel is not talking about two people but simply presenting two descriptions of the same individual linked by the explicative use of "and." We would translate that part of the verse: "and, beheld, a watcher (that is a holy one) came down from heaven."

The linguistic characteristic in our preceding examples may also help us understand the relationship between Cyrus and Darius. The dreams were linked by the word "and" in the visions of 7:1, not separated by it. The "watcher" and "holy one" are references to the same person, again linked not separated by "and." Following the same pattern, the title of Darius the Mede was included in the name of Cyrus the Persian. These descriptions are two ways of describing the same man, and not an attempt to separate them. We would say, "So this Daniel prospered in the reign of Darius, that is in the reign of Cyrus the Persian."

There is also scriptural evidence which associates Cyrus with Darius the Mede. In the first verse of chapter eleven, the Hebrew and English scriptures state Daniel's living in "**the first year of Darius the Mede**," while this verse in two of the Greek versions (Septuagint and Theodotian) report that Daniel is living in the "**first year of Cyrus**." Baldwin presents the idea that "This suggests that the Greek translator knew of the double name, and preferred to use the one that was better known to avoid confusing his readers."⁶¹ No matter what the reason, the same person is referred to as both Cyrus and Darius in different translations of the Bible.

The book of Daniel also gives other hints as to the identity of Darius. In chapter six Darius makes a decree **"Then king Darius wrote unto all people, nations, and languages, that dwell in all the earth; Peace be multiplied unto you."** (v. 25) If Darius were a simple governor of Babylon with the label of king for that region, would it be possible for him to make a declaration to "all the earth?" No but Cyrus, and Cyrus alone, as "king of lands" who ruled the entire empire could certainly do so.

William H. Shea published an interesting article in the Andrews University Seminary Studies in 1991.⁶² In it, he lists several events from Daniel which are clarified and explained by the identification of Cyrus as Darius the Mede. The next section will be a summary from Shea's article.

Shea explains that the event which allows for his new analysis is the result of a publication by the British Museum. They acquired and translated a number of contract tablets, which are normally dated in the year of the king which is ruling at the time the contract is executed. These contracts provide a chronology which allows the identification of who was considered to be king, and during which period he ruled.

The first topic addressed by Shea was whether Cambyses was considered king of Babylon, and when. Shea reports, "with this new evidence in hand, there can be no question about it: Cambyses ruled Babylon with Cyrus from 1/1, in the spring of 538 B.C., until sometime between IX/25 and X/1 of that same year. At that time, the contract tablets drop Cambyses' name and transfer his title, "king of Babylon," to Cyrus. (p. 237)

This, in fact, answers two questions. Some had considered Cambyses a candidate for Darius, which possibility is eliminated by this discovery. Second, it confirms that the title of king of Babylon was indeed held by Cyrus.

It also eliminates Gubaru II from consideration. If Cambyses and Cyrus were acting as co-regents, there is no room for another. Gubaru I died, and would probably not have had time to accomplish all of the acts attributed to Darius.

We have mentioned the inscriptions of Nabonidus and his mother found in Harran. On that inscription, Nabonidus makes reference to the "king of the Medes" in the year 546 B. C. This is well after the fall of Astyages, and it is commonly believed that it refers to Cyrus and confirms his title as Median king. Shea agrees with the basic premise, but diverges on the process involved in arriving at it. (p. 240)

Shea says that Gubaru I (Ugbaru) ruled in Babylon until the arrival several days later of Cyrus. At that time, Cyrus was given the kingship which Gubaru I had held in trust. This possibly explains Daniel 5:31 which states that Darius "received the kingdom." Cyrus, at that time, did receive the kingdom from Gubaru. (pp. 244, 245) Gubaru I died soon after the arrival of Cyrus.

Daniel states that Darius installed the sub-governors in Babylon, but who would have done this, considering that Gubaru I died so quickly? It is likely that this was accomplished between the death of Gubaru, who had probably begun the selection process, and the installation of Cambyses some time later. While the process was probably begun by Gubaru, Cyrus was the only reasonable candidate for the accomplishment of this task. (pp. 245, 246)

The subject of Darius' first decree has an interesting interpretation. Darius states that for a period of thirty days no one can pray to anyone but Darius. A section of the Nabonidus Chronicle may shed some light on this, it says, "the gods of Akkad which Nabonidus had made come down to Babylon, were returned to their sacred cities." During that period worshippers could not visit or pray to their traveling gods, and it is possible that the enemies of Daniel used this excuse to approach Darius/Cyrus. They may well have presented it as a way to provide a measure of religious security to the people whose deities were unavailable during that time.

What seems like a very strange request to us today, probably didn't appear quite so unusual in that context. It could also be speculated that they never intended to enforce the decree with anyone but Daniel, so it wouldn't have made any difference to them. The Cyrus Cylinder also provides an interesting insight into this event, as it states that because of Cyrus the people "had all been spared damage and disaster, and they worshipped his (very) name." (pp. 246, 247) The Cyrus Cylinder actually states that the people of Babylon may have worshiped Cyrus after he liberated the city. This is another strong historical confirmation of Daniel.

These points, combined with our previous comments on Cyrus as Darius the Mede, provide some very interesting possibilities. They cannot be considered proof that Cyrus indeed was the mysterious Darius the Mede, but they do cast serious doubts on the contention that Darius was an imaginary character created by a second-century Jew. The chart at the end of this section, used with permission of the *Andrews University Seminary Studies*, will help us understand the sequence of events.

I would like to reinforce this final point. The idea that the author of Daniel used the character of Darius the Mede by accident or in error does not ring true. There is ample evidence from scripture that it was Cyrus who conquered Babylon. In fact, Cyrus was revered and honored as a servant of God in returning the exiled Jews to their covenant lands. Isaiah 44:28 says, **"That saith of Cyrus, He is my shepherd, and shall perform all my pleasure: even saying to Jerusalem, Thou shalt be built; and to the temple, Thy foundation shall be laid."**

There are numerous references in the books of 2 Chronicles, Ezra, and Isaiah to Cyrus and his aid to the children of Israel. Cyrus was considered by most Hebrews to be a hero to the Jewish nation and this, for me, means his inclusion or exclusion could not have been made in error. The author either wanted to have a glaring mistake in his work, or knew that his reference was correct. I believe the mention of Darius in his role of conqueror of Babylon stands as an internal testimony to the personal knowledge of the political situation in Babylon by Daniel's author.

The Issues from Criticism 6:

1 – Who was Darius the Mede, was he a real person? There is no way to prove the identity of Darius the Mede, but that is not necessary for our purposes. It is enough to demonstrate that references to Darius in the Book of Daniel could refer to several people, the most likely of which is Cyrus the Great, who's father was Persian but who's mother was a Mede. It is not inconceivable that Cyrus, grandson of the Median king, would also have a Median name - Darius. The Book of Esther clearly indicates that a name used in the Bible may not be the same as the commonly known throne name, Ahasuerus being better known historically as Xerxes. There is also enough evidence to indicate that Darius could have been a real person, and that his mention cannot be considered a major contradiction to the authenticity of Daniel.

Diagram 1

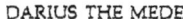

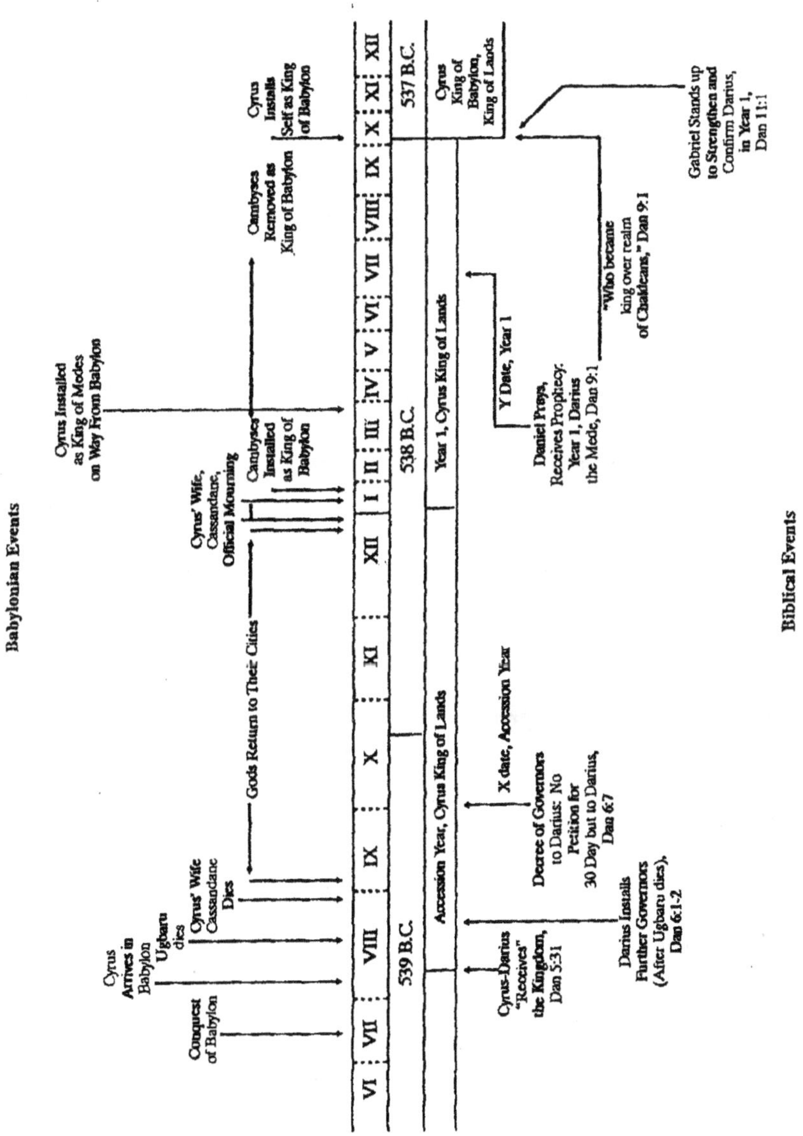

Section 4: General Historical Arguments

We will first address one of the important historical questions raised by critics, "Why is there no mention of Daniel before the second-century B.C.?" This lack of mention is known as "an argument from silence." According to the late date proponents, history is completely silent with regards to Daniel. Since there is no independent confirmation of Daniel's existence, then he probably didn't exist. However, even if it is true that no existing sources mention Daniel, this does not mean that he did not exist. There is no reference to Belshazzar outside of Daniel, and his existence has only been recently confirmed. It is possible that no one had reason to write about him, or more likely is that any references to him were lost through the centuries.

On its own, an argument from silence is very weak and could never support any theory regarding authorship by itself. However, it can be employed to support other, more substantial arguments as is the case with Daniel. The substance of this assertion is that according to the critics, there are several places where they believe some specific mention of Daniel should have been made. One of these places is Ezekiel.

Ezekiel, however, presents an interesting problem because it does mention someone named "Danel" or "Daniel" three times. This problem is overcome by critics by claiming that Ezekiel's reference could not possibly be to the Daniel we are discussing. Pfeiffer outlines the question this way:

> The Daniel of Ezekiel could conceivably be identical with that of Ras Shamra, but hardly with the hero of our book [Daniel] who, being at least ten years younger than Ezekiel, could hardly be classed with Noah; moreover, in 591 and 586 when Ezekiel was writing those passages, our

Daniel had barely begun his career, which extended from 606 to 535 according to the explicit statements of our book. Nor could our hero be identified with a contemporary of Ezra and Nehemiah, since he must have died long before -- assuming for the moment that he was a historical character.[63]

The insistence that the quotes from Ezekiel, which does refer to Daniel, could not be referring to the Daniel of the Bible is based on two points. First, that Ezekiel's quote refers to an historical figure, probably "Danel" from Ugaritic literature. Second, that Ezekiel could not or would not have been talking about Daniel from Baylon because Daniel would have been unknown to Ezekiel. Even if Ezekiel had known about Daniel, being a contemporary he would not have been able to attain the stature necessary to be mentioned with Job and Noah.

As we examine the first by question by Pfeiffer, stating that Ezekiel was referring to someone else, we note that this quote mentions a Daniel (or Danel in Ugaritic) of Ras Shamra as the likely source for this reference. Since vowels were not used in Hebrew at this time, either name could have been the one used by Ezekiel. It could have been either name.

To provide some background, Ras Shamra (Ugarit) was a city/kingdom on the Mediterranean coast and far north of Judah. It has recently been explored, and a number of interesting texts were found there. In one of them was the story of a king called Danel. Danel was a pagan, who offered sacrifice to Bel and other Canaanite gods. In fact, the god Bel championed Danel's quest, to be given a son, before the other gods.

As mentioned, the critics believed him to be the Daniel referred to in Ezeki(14:14, 20; 28:3). This connection is necessary, because "Danel" offers critics the only known alternative, other than the Daniel credited for the Biblical book, for the quotes from Ezekiel that we are discussing. If it is accurate to assume that critics began their analysis with the supposition that the Daniel of the Book of Daniel didn't exist. It as assumed, then, that Ezekiel's quotes must have referenced someone else. The discovery of the Ugaritic stories provides the most attractive alternative.

Let's look quickly at the context of the first example. Ezekiel 14:12-14 states that God's judgment would not be averted, even by the intervention of righteous men:

> **The word of the LORD came again to me, saying, Son of man, when the land sinneth against me by trespassing grievously, then will I stretch out mine hand upon it, and will break the staff of the bread thereof, and will send famine upon it, and will cut off man and beast from it: Though these three men, Noah, Daniel, and Job, were in it, they should deliver but their own souls by their righteousness, saith the Lord GOD.**

Ezekiel is saying even righteous men such as those mentioned could only save themselves, and not the nation because of its wickedness. The assumption we would be forced to accept if Ezekiel is talking about "Danel," is that a pagan king, a worshipper of Bel, would be held up as an example of righteousness along with Noah and Job.

I find this suggestion to be untenable, and believe that Ezekiel, or any prophet, would be very reluctant to base righteous behavior on the moral teachings from a pagan legend. The actions of the

Canaanite gods Bel, Kothar, Anath, and El are integral to the story of Danel. I again find it inconceivable to suggestion that Ezekiel believed them to be true, and I must reject any suggestion that he used them in his prophecies in God's name.

Now let's examine this chapter to see if we can discover any addional information, which might help us to identify another source of the reference. Ezekiel is speaking out against specific problems existing within the nation of Judah. Verses 3-5 of chapter 14 will help us identify the behavior which has brought this rebuke:

> **These men have set up their idols in their heart, and put the stumblingblock of their iniquity before their face: should I be enquired of at all by them? Therefore speak unto them, and say unto them, Thus saith the Lord GOD; Every man of the house of Israel that setteth up his idols in his heart, and putteth the stumblingblock of his iniquity before his face, and cometh to the prophet; I the LORD will answer him that cometh according to the multitude of his idols; That I may take the house of Israel in their own heart, because they are all estranged from me through their idols.**

The Jewish nation is being chastised for doing iniquity, and for setting up idols and worshiping them with their hearts. This further diminishes the likelihood of the Danel of Ugaritic legend being referenced by Ezekiel. It makes no sense whatsoever to use an idol worshipper as an example intended to inspire the people not to worship idols.

Who, about this time, *was* known for refusing to worship idols? There is no doubt that the stories of Shadrach, Meshach, and Abednego's refusal to worship the idol could and would have reached Jerusalem. There is no certain way of dating the relative events being discussed, but if we assume that the events from Daniel chapters 2 and 3 are true, the news of these miraculous events would have certainly been carried immediately to Jews everywhere. If we are looking for a basis for Ezekiel's message, the devout behavior of Daniel and his friends is much more probable than the pagan example proposed by the book's critics.

As an aside, I found this entire criticism amusing. Boiled down to its basic elements, the critics argue: "Why didn't Ezekiel mention Daniel if they were contemporaries?" When supporters point out that the name Daniel is mentioned, critics then complain. "It couldn't be the prophet Daniel, they were contemporaries."

Again, the entire argument appears based on the preexisting premise that Daniel could not have existed. Being mentioned by a contemporary is considered proof that a person existed, except for Daniel.

The second argument against Daniel is based on the assumption that Ezekiel could not have been familiar with Daniel, who had been carried away into exile many years before. While this is suggested, I have never seen any arguments made, or information given, which would support the assertion. This argument must be considered so obvious that no support is required.

As self-evident as they consider this point, I would like to give it a more critical examination. This assertion rests on the idea that the Jewish nation and the Babylonian nation were isolated pockets of civilization, existing in virtual isolation from each other. I have to disagree. I believe this assertion is contrary to fact.

The commercial interests of these communities alone would have necessitated regular contact between these two commercial centers, as well as those in Egypt. Politically and economically, Israel would have relied on the power and wealth of these to centers. It is extremely short sighted to believe that commercial leaders in Jerusalem would not be regularly updated on events in the seat of government, whose decisions would have such a profound impact on their operations.

We must remember, also, that at this time Judah was a part of the Babylonian Empire. It is a mistake, therefore, to assume there was not a regular flow of information between the capital of this province and the center of the Empire it was a part of. The negotiation over tribute and requests for legal rulings would have necessitated routine communication.

How shortsighted would it be to assert that Nebuchadnezzar, who was forced to invade Judah three times, would not maintain regular contact with this troublesome nation? Even more doubtful is that Judah, having been invaded by Babylon, and under a near-constant threat of invasion, would not be carefully and constantly monitoring what was going on in Babylon.

If Daniel were elevated to a high position of leadership in the Babylonian court, this fact also would be well known to the Jewish population of Jerusalem. Indeed, if Daniel and his friends were in positions of leadership in the capital city, then it would be almost certain that representatives from Jerusalem would have had direct contact with them. Not only would he have been known, but sought out for aid with any legal or commercial issues to be dealt with in Babylon. Daniel would be precisely the example of faithfulness being rewarded that Ezekiel would want to present. Dr. Leon J. Wood offers the following observation:

> It should be noted that Ezekiel was Daniel's contemporary, arriving as a captive in Babylon eight years later. By this time, Daniel would have already held the important position he attained in the

government, and Ezekiel, it may be assumed, would have made inquiry, on arrival, regarding the young Judean who had risen to such a height so quickly. He likely thought that first that one would have to cater to pagan ways to do this. But Ezekiel clearly had discovered differently and was sufficiently impressed by what he had found to mention Daniel in parallel with Noah and Job as a great man of righteousness. This fact is still more remarkable when one recognizes that persons who live in a prior generation tend to stand out more brilliantly than contemporaries.[64]

While I agree with the sentiments, I do not agree with all of the details in Dr. Wood's analysis. I do not believe Ezekiel would have had to wait until arriving at Babylon to hear of Daniel, his friends, or their experiences and blessings. I believe these stories, once we assume they could be true, would have quickly become common knowledge to both the Jews in Babylonian exile, and then to those remaining in Judah. Daniel would therefore be a logical example of faithfulness when confronted by pagan beliefs, a perfect choice for Ezekiel's admonition.

There are also other topics to be discussed, but I again want to point out that verse 20 of this chapter in Ezekiel also supports my theory, by continuing with the theme that righteousness brings deliverance. While this question will probably never be resolved, it is still unlikely that a pagan figure of legend would be believed or repeated by Ezekiel, or be used within the context in which it is recorded by him. This is especially true because the Book of Daniel itself offers a very powerful example.

I believe that this provides us with another example where the conclusion is what determines the interpretation of the evidence, instead of an examination of the evidence leading to a conclusion. The idea that Daniel could not have been mentioned by Ezekiel, when seriously examined, may not be as objectionable as critics present. I personally believe that if given these two individuals as the only candidates for the Ezekiel reference, the Jewish Daniel is the more likely and better fits the context of the verse. In fact, I suspect when given an impartial analysis, that "Danel" from Ras Shamra would not be given serious consideration at all if it weren't required as an alternative to Daniel the prophet.

Another omission from historical reference is often represented as proof that Daniel did not exist until the second-century B.C. The writings of ben Sira, found in the Apocryphal book of Ecclesiasticus, are universally accepted and cited as proof by late date proponents. Again, we will begin with the observations of Driver:

> Jesus, the son of Sirach (writing c. 200 B.C.), in his enumeration of Israelitish worthies c. 44-50, though he mentions Isaiah, Jeremiah, Ezekiel, and (collectively) the Twelve Minor Prophets, is silent as to Daniel. [65]

The assumption in Driver's quote being that Daniel didn't exist, and therefore, could not have been listed by ben Sira.
These comments reference the list found in the book of Ecclesiasticus 44, which lists well known heroes from Jewish history. The Interpreters Concise Commentary claims:

> He makes no mention of Daniel, evidently because he does not know of the book about him. About 180 [B.C.] Jeshua ben

> Sira lists the heroes of the faith from Enoch, Noah and Abraham through Nehemiah (Ecclesiasticus 44).[66]

Both of these quotes leave the impression that all the Jewish heroes are listed, and Daniel is the only one omitted. This is not the case. There are others who were likewise skipped by ben Sira, including Ezra, Gideon, Saul, Asa and Jehoshaphat. In light of these omissions, we must wonder how much, if any, significance should be attached to the exclusion of Daniel? Ben Sira, believed to have been an extreme religious conservative, may not have approved of Daniel for any number of reasons. Daniel was a "Chaldean," he also administered affairs exclusively in Babylon, was part of the administration of pagan kings who destroyed the temple and exiled the Jews, any of which would explain Daniel's exclusion from the list.

Ben Sira did not list all of the prominent Israelites, excluding important figures such as Jehoshaphat and Ezra. The omission of Ezra was interesting, because Ezra was also from the Babylonian exile. In fact, when we look at figures which were prominent during this time, there are other omissions. Haggai and Zechariah are also missing from this list. These three were extremely important for the establishment of Judah and the construction of the temple after the exile. The books of Ezra, Haggai and Zechariah are actual books of scripture. These books are found in the Bible, while Ecclesiasticus is not.

I find it puzzling, and a little frustrating, that this question has not been given more consideration – either by the critics of Daniel or by its supporters. In fact, I have never read anything written which highlights the other prominent omissions in Ecclesiasticus relating to the Babylonian exile. The fact that such a significant number of prominent people from this period and geography are excluded must certainly raise the possibility that Daniel's omission has absolutely nothing to do with the existence of this specific book or its author.

It is very possible that ben Sira had objections to Daniel for any one of a number of reasons. We have just noted that three other names from the exilic period, all of whom have books accepted as scripture, are missing. Daniel's absence from ben Sira's list is far from conclusive evidence that he did not exist.

The next difficulty arises because of the placement of Daniel in the Writings section of the Hebrew Bible. The Interpreters One-Volume Commentary states: "The fact that the book in the Hebrew Bible is placed among the Writings rather than the Prophets indicates a late date; if it had been in existence before c. 200 B.C. it probably would have been included among the Prophets."[67]

The reasoning for this is two part. First, if those who compiled the Hebrew Scriptures really believed that Daniel was a prophet, they would have included him in the section of the Hebrew Bible known as "the Prophets." Second, Daniel was also written so late it didn't qualify as a prophetic book. Both of these reasons are used as justification for the argument that it is a product of the second-century B.C.

Before we address Daniel's placement in the Writings of the Hebrew scripture, it is important to note that Daniel *is* included with the Prophets in both the Septuagint (LXX) and English Bibles. The assumption that the Hebrew Bible must be correct is curious, since the Septuagint is much older. One wonders if the selection of the Hebrew Bible as authoritative on this particular matter did not rely mainly on the fact that it was the one which supported their arguments regarding Daniel.

However, let us examine the possible reasons for the location of Daniel in the "Hagiographa," or Writings. The first reason given was that Daniel was not considered a prophet. This is not really a problem. The fact is, that Daniel was *not* a prophet in the traditional Jewish sense. Jeremiah 18:5-12 explains the role of a prophet. Verses 8 and 10 specifically summarize the traditional role of a prophet. "**If that nation, against whom I have pronounced, turn from their evil, I will repent of the evil that I thought to do unto them. If it do evil in my sight, that it obey not my voice, then I will repent of the good, wherewith I said I would benefit them.** "

Prophets (the voice of God) were called by God to minister to His people and to call them back to the path of righteousness. Daniel, on the other hand, was a bureaucrat. His principal prophetic gift was interpreting dreams, often those of pagan kings, and predicting the course of the gentile nations. There were some extremely valuable teachings included in his ministry, but he never did fill the traditional role of prophet.

Driver actually helps us understand this point. "It is remarkable also that Daniel--so unlike the prophets generally--should display no interest in the welfare, or prospects of his contemporaries."[68] This feature of Daniel's writing, an almost complete lack of interest in the Jews of his time, was certainly a contributing factor to his removal from the prophets in the Hebrew scripture.

I hope you noticed that my last statement referenced Daniel's "removal" from the prophets, because it is my assertion that before the Proto-Massoretic/Proto-Rabbinical standardization, beginning about the time of Christ, that Daniel was indeed considered a prophet, and his teachings were included with them. This is supported by it's inclusion with the prophets in the Septuagint.

I will briefly explain the reference to Proto-Massoretic and Proto-Rabbinical texts, with a more complete treatment included in the linguistic analysis of Daniel. That section will provide a more detailed explanation, especially regarding the question of dating the book, but some information will help our current discussion.

In the last few centuries before Christ, the Jewish people had three religious and cultural centers, Jerusalem, Babylon and Egypt. It is estimated that there were more Jews in the city of Alexandria, Egypt than in all of Palestine during this period. The scriptures were present in each, and each center developed a distinct literary tradition regarding the scriptures. In Egypt, for example, the scriptures eventually had to be translated into Greek because few Jews actually spoke Hebrew. Even in Palestine some scholars believe that much of the religious instruction was conducted in Greek, since Hebrew was not the common language of the people.

About the time of Christ, there was an effort to standardize the scriptural texts, at least in Jerusalem. A Babylonian Rabbi named Hillel is considered one of the likely forces behind this effort, and many of the 'canonical' versions of the sacred writings were actually of the Babylonian tradition. These scriptural versions, which were ultimately chosen and accepted, were called books of the Rabbinic Tradition. The earlier versions of these books which were eventually considered official, again in the time of Hillel, are called Proto-Rabbinic.

The most common name for this collection of books is "Proto-Massoretic," or pre-Massoretic. The Masoretes, about the 5th century A.D., revised the Hebrew Bible to make it easier to read, and in the process fixed for good the body of scripture. The actual selection of books, however, had really been accomplished during the first-century A.D. through the efforts of Rabbinic scholars and the conference at Jamnia.

This counsel occurred after the destruction of Jerusalem when a group of Rabbis who had supported the Romans during the war of 70 A.D., were allowed to set up a school at Jamnia. One of the reasons for this council in Jamnia was to meet the threat of the growing

Christian movement. It was at this time, or possibly at the time of Hillel, when the rabbinic scholars chose their official versions, that Daniel was probably removed from the Prophets and assigned to the section known as Writings.

The "Writings" was the section designated for those books of scripture considered to be literary and historical in nature. These were in contrast to the books of Moses or the books of the prophets. A book in the Writings was considered scripture, but not of a prophetic nature or not written by someone considered to be a prophet.

Even with its ultimate exclusion from the prophetic section of the Hebrew scripture, this may not reflect the actual, previous status of the book of Daniel in Israel. It will certainly be very helpful for us to ascertain the prevailing opinions regarding Daniel in the various religious communities prior to the selection of the Proto-Rabbinic and Proto-Massoretic books. One place which illustrates the book's status is in the New Testament itself. What was the opinion of those living in Jerusalem at that time? Did they consider Daniel to be a prophet? Let's look at a couple of examples:

> Matt. 24:15 **When ye therefore shall see the abomination of desolation, spoken of by Daniel the prophet, stand in the holy place,**
> Mark 13:14 **But when ye shall see the abomination of desolation, spoken of by Daniel the prophet, standing where it ought not,**

These quotes indicate that Christ and the two apostles here cited, considered Daniel to be a prophet.

The Dead Sea Scrolls offer more insight into this period. What was the opinion within the community at Qumran regarding Daniel? William Brownlee writes: "One cannot carefully study the Qumran literature without noting the pervasive influence of Daniel upon the thought and language of the sect. Whatever the theory of canonicity, for all practical purposes Daniel was authoritative."[69] This means they considered Daniel to be a prophet and his book to be scripture, probably centuries before Christ.

The Anchor Bible Commentary on Daniel deals directly with this question:

> [quoting from Qumran text 4Q174] "it is written in the Book of Daniel the prophet." These words are then followed by quotations of Dan 12:10 and 11:32. This Qumran text is to be dated ca. 30-1 B.C. It seems, from this evidence, that the Essenes of the Qumran community considered Daniel as one of the prophets and presumably placed his book among the prophetic books rather than among the Writings as did the later rabbis.[70]

A final example should suffice. Josephus was a Jewish Historian during the first-century A.D. He records the general feeling of the Jewish scholars and people of that day regarding the status of Daniel. His comments are found in his book *Antiquities of the Jews*, Book 10 Chapter 11:

> Moreover, he took *Daniel the prophet* (italics added), and carried him with him into Media, and honored him very greatly (paragraph 4)

> But it is fit to give an account of what this man [Daniel] did, which is most admirable to hear, for he was so happy as to have strange revelations made to him, and those as to one of the greatest of the prophets, insomuch, that while he was

> alive he had the esteem and applause both of the kings and of the multitude; and now he is dead, he retains a remembrance that will never fail, for the several books that he wrote and left behind him are still read by us till this time; and from them we believe that Daniel conversed with God; for he did not only prophesy of future events, as did the other prophets, but he also determined the time of their accomplishment. And while prophets used to foretell misfortunes, and on that account were disagreeable both to the kings and to the multitude, Daniel was to them a prophet of good things, and this to such a degree, that by the agreeable nature of his predictions, he procured the goodwill of all men; and by the accomplishment of them, he procured the belief of their truth, and the opinion of [a sort of] divinity for himself, among the multitude. (Paragraph 7)

Josephus not only considered Daniel to be a prophet, but to be one of "the greatest of the prophets."

There was an almost universal acceptance by the Jewish community, from the second-century B.C. to the first-century A.D., of Daniel as a prophet. As mentioned before the Jews in Egypt considered him a prophet, and included his book with the other Prophets in their body of scripture. Why then, was Daniel included in the Writings of the Hebrew Bible?

We will provide possible answers to this question shortly, but first let us consider the second reason for assuming a late date for Daniel. Many believe that all late books – written after about 400 B.C. – were not included with the prophets. Because of this, they placed Daniel in the writings because, according to the critics, they knew it was not written during the exile but much later.

This argument relies on the assumption that its supposed late date was the reason it was included in the Writings. However, this argument may not be important. If the Writings were to have included the historical books, then that is where Daniel belongs. The question of when it was written may not have been a factor at all. The final placement does not mean that those making the decision didn't believe Daniel was a prophet or didn't write the book. Its location only indicates that his book was mainly of an historical instead of a prophetic nature.

Despite assertions by the proponents of the late date that the early rabbis made their decisions on Daniel because of its late date and questionable authorship, they are probably incorrect. Remember, we have just demonstrated the almost universal acceptance throughout the Jewish world of Daniel as a prophet. The fact that they quote the book of Daniel and attribute those prophetic quotes directly to him, indicate they believe the book was written by him and was authoritative.

I believe one of the contributing factors to it being placed in the Writings was the use of Daniel in the Christian community. Daniel foretold the coming of the Messiah, and some suggest that the Christians were using Daniel as a witness to the mission of Christ. While the Rabbis might not have been so bold as to remove a sacred book, they may have included it in the Writings instead of the Prophets to diminish the effectiveness of its use by the Christians. Again, this may or may not have played a factor, because I maintain that the book of Daniel could justifiably have been placed in the Writings based on its subject matter and presentation alone.

It should be pointed out, however, that there never was any discussion of Daniel not belonging in the body of scripture:

> Although it is widely held that soon after the destruction of the Temple the Rabbis held a canonical convention at the rabbinical academy at Yavneh (Jamnia), on the coast south of what is today Tel Aviv, the textual evidence does not support the claim. In fact, the final catalog of the biblical collection was fixed except for those few books of the Writings, the late date of which left them in question. Thus, the Rabbis debated only about a few books, namely, Song of Songs and Ecclesiastes, and perhaps Esther. Because mishnaic Judaism had already inherited a tradition, predating the Yavnean period and ordaining which books were part of the biblical canon, the Rabbis at Yavneh had only to make a few final rulings to complete the corpus. [71]

At this point in history, inside the Jewish community, Daniel was not one of the books whose authenticity was being questioned.

One point presented in the previous quote should be emphasized. There were a number of books for which a late date was suspected. These books were scrutinized, and some were accepted while others were abandoned. Daniel was never questioned. Many other books, some associated with Daniel, were excluded base in part on these arguments regarding authorship and date. The books of the Apocrypha were all excluded from Hebrew scripture. If the scholars of the first-century B.C. had believed that the book of Daniel itself was not authentic, they would not have included it either. Being only decades removed from the supposed date of composition, it is not credible to suggest they would not have known it to be a recent work, and equally incredible to assume they would ignore this and placed it in the scriptures in spite of this.

Historically, there are a number of problems which arise if a late date is assumed for Daniel. The stories of Daniel would not have appealed to the entire population, even in Palestine:

> It should be emphasized that the religious outlook of the book is that of only one segment of Judaism in the second century B.C., viz. the Jews whose spokesmen were like the authors and editors of the books of Daniel and I-II Maccabees. Not all Jews agreed with this unbending position. Many, doubtless in good faith, attempted to accommodate their Jewish belief and practice to the spirit and necessities of the day.[72]

This doesn't quite cover this question. Daniel teaches concepts such as the resurrection of the dead (Chapter 12), a concept which was energetically opposed by powerful elements of the Jewish community. I find it difficult to believe that a recently prepared book, striving for acceptance in the troubled environment of Palestine, could have been universally accepted while teaching such a divisive doctrine. One only need remember the example of Paul, a few years from the suggested late date of the book's acceptance, after his arrest in the temple:

> **But when Paul perceived that the one part were Sadducees, and the other Pharisees, he cried out in the council, Men and brethren, I am a Pharisee, the son of a Pharisee: of the hope and resurrection of the dead I am called in question. And when there arose a great dissension, the chief captain, fearing lest Paul should have been**

pulled in pieces of them, commanded the soldiers to go down, and to take him by force from among them, and to bring him into the castle. (Acts 23: 6, 7, 10)

Paul was almost killed because he believed in the resurrection. I can only assume that a work which suddenly appeared, introducing the resurrection and other controversial topics, would have encountered the same type of resistance.

While there were topics which some factions in the Jewish communities would have resisted, there are things in Daniel that all pious Jews would have probably rejected outright if the book had not already established itself before the second-century B.C. There are several historical elements in Daniel which contradict or oppose what is written in other books. We need only look at the first verse for examples. Daniel claims Nebuchadnezzar became king in the third year of Jehoiakim, while Jeremiah says it was the fourth. In other examples, Daniel claims that Darius the Mede conquered Babylon, while numerous passages (2 Ch. 36:22-23, Ezra 1:1-8, etc.) state that it was Cyrus. Daniel suggests that Belshazzar ruled following the reign of king of Nebuchadnezzar, while Jeremiah and 2 Kings both state it was Evilmerodach. There are other examples, which put the book of Daniel at odds with what would certainly have been considered more authoritative books. Yet, nowhere is there any indication that the authenticity of Daniel was questioned, or that it was considered anything other than the product of a sixth-century B.C. prophet.

When you consider all of the reasons some, or all of the Jews would have had for rejecting Daniel, it is very difficult to understand why it was never challenged. If it had been written just decades earlier, it would have been rejected based on its historical contradiction of other, established works of scripture.

Section 5: Linguistic Arguments

This part of our analysis may be a little more complex than the others. I do not read the original languages of the texts, and will in advance qualify my remarks with the admission that I am unable to comment on the detailed evaluations of Daniel's linguistic features. The discussion will therefore focus on the conclusions of the various experts, while omitting detailed evaluations of the data upon which those conclusions are based. Besides, a detailed evaluation of the linguistic points would clearly be outside the scope of this work. We will try to provide an overview of the field, and relate that to the topic at hand.

Despite the complexity and risks of this study, we discover that the language found within the texts of Daniel can provide valuable insights into its date and place of origin. In the past, the language of Daniel was interpreted as a powerful confirmation of its second-century B.C. composition. However, as more documents and texts have been discovered, the Dead Sea Scrolls being the most dramatic example, the answer to this question is much less certain.

This discussion will be much easier to understand if we provide some historical background. We know that in 598/7 B.C., Nebuchadnezzar did destroy Jerusalem and take many of its inhabitants into captivity. While few remained in Palestine, many did flee to safety in Egypt, which had once been Judah's ally. Over the years, and for a variety of reasons, the Jewish population in Egypt grew. This was especially true after the establishment of Alexandria. Egypt and Alexandria became a place where the Jews would be protected from the direct consequences of war, and enjoy a robust economic environment.

Another relatively secure place for the Jewish people was in the heart of the Persian Empire, especially Babylon. They had established themselves in Babylon during the captivity, under relatively favorable circumstances. They were free to continue their religious practices and, since they posed no threat to the rulers of the land, were basically ignored politically.

The one place where the Jews had to struggle to survive was in Judah. They were in constant conflict with their neighbors, and this was economically the least hospitable of the three centers of Jewish civilization. The land and its growing seasons were limited, so there was no reliable agricultural base from which to establish a strong economy or government. Judah and Palestine were also a frequent battleground for the competing monarchs of the Ptolemy and Seleucids families.

The result was that a single "Jewish culture" did not exist. There were actually three centers of culture, which were centered in Jerusalem, Babylon and Alexandria/Egypt. Each developed their own distinct religious traditions reflecting the physical and spiritual needs of their environment. They also developed their own traditions regarding the importance and composition of the scriptures.

An understanding of the process by which the book of Daniel was incorporated into the text of the various translations of the Bible may provide us with some ideas regarding its date of origin. Traditionally, it was believed that the Greek bible, the Septuagint (LXX), was a translation of the Hebrew texts which eventually formed the Jewish scriptures. This theory, however, is no longer adequate to explain the variety of ancient texts now available.

The Anchor Bible Commentary on Daniel provides an interesting overview of this question:

> On the basis of recent data from Qumran caves and elsewhere, F. M. Cross has

> attempted to prove that complex Hebrew textual traditions paralleled the development of the various Greek recensions. Each sequence in one had its correspondent in the other. Cross has argued for the existence of three Hebrew textual traditions: the Egyptian, the Palestinian, and the Babylonian. Each of these has its reflex in the Greek recensions: The Egyptian tradition is transmitted in the Old Greek (LXX); the Palestinian in the Proto Lucianic recension; and the Babylonian, which had moved back to Palestine during the Hasmonean or Herodian period, in the Proto-Theodotionic or *kaige* recension.[73]

As I mentioned previously, there were different textual traditions in each center of Jewish culture and religion. In these centers, the development of the sacred texts varied, and can be to some extent identified.

It will help in the further discussion of this material if we illustrate the sequence implied in the previous quote. This will be a simplified, possibly over-simplified representation, but the limitations on this topic have already been stated. The development progressed after this manner:

Diagram 2

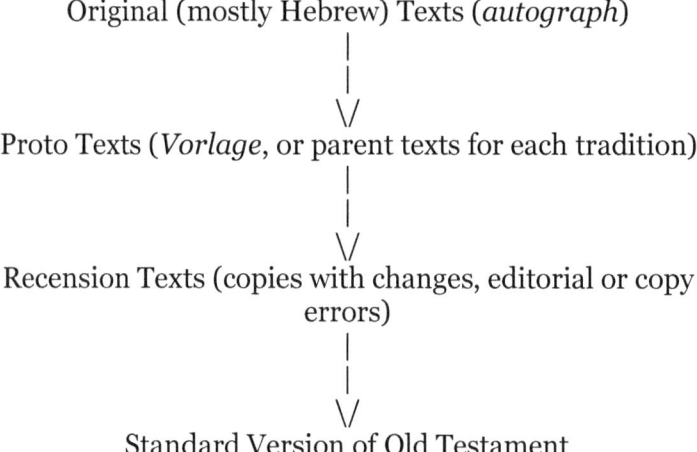

Original (mostly Hebrew) Texts (*autograph*)
↓
Proto Texts (*Vorlage*, or parent texts for each tradition)
↓
Recension Texts (copies with changes, editorial or copy errors)
↓
Standard Version of Old Testament

This diagram is a simplified representation of a process applied to both the Hebrew and Greek versions of the sacred texts which formed the Bible. Allow me to explain a little more about the quote from the *Anchor Bible Commentary*. It lists the three textual traditions, the Egyptian, Lucian, and the Theodotian. The Bible of the early Christians was the Septuagint (LXX), the first standardized version of the Old Testament in Greek. As the Christian church grew, this became a problem because the LXX had many differences from the Hebrew (Proto-Rabbinic/Massoretic) version.

These differences were at first considered to be translational differences, or errors, on the part of the scholars who did the original translations into Greek. Now, however, most scholars agree that instead of being translation problems, the Greek translators were actually working from different parent copies (Vorlage) than those which became the Hebrew Bible.

T. J. Meadowcroft's book comparing the Aramaic and Greek versions of Daniel asserts that the major differences between the divergent versions of the Old Testament in general, and Daniel in particular, are indeed the result of different source documents. He explains that "it seems inherently unlikely therefore that the Septuagintal translator of Daniel would have been translating a MT-like[Massoretic Text] *Vorlage* at points where the versions diverge substantially."[74] The same observation is made by Menahem Mansoor in his textbook on the Dead Sea Scrolls:

> We also know that the Septuagint was made from a Hebrew text existing at that time and that therefore the differences between the Septuagint and the Masoretic text are not due to errors on the part of the Greek translators.[75]

The differences were in the actual documents they were

translated from, indicating that indeed there were significant differences in Biblical texts.

These are just two of the many examples, which serve to explain the diagram above, and those which are to follow. They show that the different Greek versions of Daniel originally existed as separate Hebrew texts, and were not simply different translations of the same text.

The LXX text is reported to have been written in Alexandria around 250 B.C. The traditions surrounding its creation are not germane to our question and will not be discussed, but it is generally accepted that it was translated by and for the Jewish community in Egypt.

The *Anchor Bible Commentary* provides a comprehensive analysis of Daniel. The commentary indicates its analysis, at least in part, is based on the work of F. M. (Frank Moore) Cross. Cross himself provides an excellent example of this developmental process by explaining the development of the book of Samuel where the "resources are particularly rich."[76] The following list describes the development of the Book of Samuel:

1. Source was edited in Palestine - mid sixth century B.C.
2. A later version was taken to Babylonian community.
3. Old Palestinian text taken to Egypt—early 3rd century B.C.
4. Each tradition (Palestinian, Babylonian, and Egyptian) develops independently, with the Palestinian (Qumran) and Egyptian more alike because they separated later (3rd vs. 6th century) than the Babylonian.
5. Hebrew text from Egypt translated into Greek – third century.
6. There was an effort to change Greek Texts to conform to Hebrew, later

Palestinian Hebrew Texts used to revise Old Greek Texts.
7. Babylonian texts later translated to Greek.

To summarize, the book of Samuel was carried off, first to Babylon then to Egypt. The text began to diverge over time, and these different sources were then translated to Greek. This period of textual isolation, revision and translation resulted in three versions of Samuel that were identifiably different. When the different versions came together, a semi-official version was selected (Palestinian Hebrew), and the other versions were modified over time to conform to that version.

As a result, all of the Hebrew traditions except one (Palestinian Hebrew) had all but disappeared by the end of the first-century A.D. This process of canonization of one specific text of each book began at the end of the first-century B.C. or early in the first-century A.D. These first standardized texts are called Rabbinic Texts because they resulted from the efforts of a group of rabbis (again, probably led by a Babylonian Rabbi named Hillel) who went through the existing versions of each book and decided which was to be accepted for use in the future. Those existing before this process are called the Proto-Rabbinic Texts; the others were ignored from that point on and eventually disappeared.

Cross used a diagram to illustrate the development of the various texts, again using the example of Samuel. I will use some of his information in the following illustration which is roughly based on his illustration:

Diagram 3

Egyptian Hebrew Texts → Old Greek Translation (Proto LXX)
                                             |
                                             |
                                            \ /
                                    Septuagint or LXX

Palestinian Hebrew Texts → Palestinian (Proto-Lucianic) Revisions
                                             |
                                             |
                                            \ /
                                        Lucianic Text

Proto-Rabbinic (Babylonian) → Proto-Theodotionic (kaige)
           Texts   Recension
             | |
             | |
            \ /   \ /
Rabbinic Recension →   Other Greek Recensions
             |
             |
            \ /
Massoretic Recension

It was the discovery of manuscripts predating the Rabbinic Recension which provided the means for arriving at the diagram above. The discovered texts, mainly the Dead Sea Scrolls, provide 'control examples' of various texts by which the changes could be measured.

    I would like to now apply the information presented in **Diagram 1** above to the creation of the LXX version of Daniel. However, **Diagram 1** does not include all of the steps required by the late date critics in the preparation of Daniel – because there was no Daniel, according to critics such as Cross, upon which to base the textual traditions. According to the proponents of the late date, the text had to be completed within the narrow period allowed by their chronology, 167-165 B.C.

Diagram 4

Completion of the Book
|
V
Book Copied and Distributed Locally
(Other copies produced and made available to the local community)
|
V
Accepted by Local Community - Palestinian/Temple Religious Leaders.
(If the Book had not been accepted in its original community, rejection would have probably precluded distribution elsewhere. This process would require a great deal of time, or a strong existing tradition.)
|
V
Revisions, Copies Produced, Book Distributed Outside of Local Community
|
V
Book Accepted In Other Communities
(Quick acceptance of a supposedly ancient book of scripture, much of which no one in that community had ever heard of, seems unreasonable.)
|
V
Book Translated
|
V
Book Copied, then distributed, in New Language
|
V
Studied, Accepted by Non-Hebrew Speaking Community, Copied, Edited
(According to many contemporary scholars, the Septuagint was not the original Greek form. The Proto-LXX, called the Old Greek, was formed and accepted before achieving its final form in the LXX.)
|
V
Final form of Septuagint Achieved

Before continuing our examination of the development of the LXX version of Daniel, I would like to address a possible point of criticism. There are many who postulate that the Aramaic stories, Chapters 2-6 of Daniel, existed as oral or written traditions long before the final version of the book was achieved. Whether this is true or not, it has no real importance for the discussion at hand. Each of the versions we are discussing contained the Hebrew sections, chapters 1, 2, 7-12. The LXX version contains the references in chapters eight, eleven and elsewhere which are used to definitively date Daniel to c. 167-165 B.C. The possibly pre-existing sections are not the problem.

The discussions on whether to accept the authority of the text of Daniel would rest as much, if not more, on these supposedly new prophetic portions of the book which could not have been familiar to them if a date of authorship of 167-165 B.C. is affirmed. As we established in the section on the unity of Daniel, we will not allow this easy way out for late date proponents. The book we are discussing, in all three traditions, included the same basic stories and prophecies, with most differences being in order and literary quality of the presentation only.

In all religious centers, once the book was completed, more copies would have to be prepared. The process of copying a book was not as simple as one might assume. If a book was considered to be scripture, the scribe believed he was copying the Word of God and special materials and preparations were usually required. These copies would then be distributed in the local community, for our purposes of discussion Palestine, who would then read, study and debate the texts before passing judgment on whether to accept them as authentic.

In Palestine, the earliest possible appearance of a final form for Daniel would probably be in 166-165 B.C., and this is likely a very generous date. The range of dates usually extends to about 165 B.C. for the completion of the text. After completion, time to prepare copies for distribution would have to be added to that. It would not be difficult to argue that the book would have first achieved complete distribution throughout the general religious community of Palestine in 164-162 B.C.

The process of writing, copying and distributing the text is very easy when compared to that required for its acceptance as scripture. There is no set formula by which we can determine the length of time required for a text to be accepted as the Word of God, but with most of the books, it is measured in generations while in Daniel's case it would have to be measured in months.

It bears repeating at this point, that the late date theory rests on the fact that many of the most significant portions of Daniel were completely unknown in the general religious community before 166 or 165 B.C. Therefore, they could not have existed as a complete work until after 167-165 B.C. We must also remember that Daniel's prophecies fail, according to the late date theory we are examining, late in the year 165 or early in year 164, when the prophecy regarding Antiochus death is proven to be wrong. We will discuss this question and others relating to possible problems with acceptance later in this paper, but critics have no way of avoiding the fact that general acceptance of this new revision could not have begun before this time.

The book would have had to be well distributed and well on its way to acceptance as scripture before any effort would have been made to carry it to the other centers of Jewish religion. It is highly unlikely that any religious Jew would take a book that had not been fully accepted as scripture in its original community and represent it as such somewhere else. If it were distributed before being fully accepted as scripture, it then would have had to undergo and successfully pass the entire process of acceptance as canon in two other locations, Egypt and Babylon.

This, in fact, may have been the case with the

deuterocanonical books of Daniel - Susanna, Bel and the Dragon, etc. They were accepted as authoritative in the Egyptian texts, but rejected in the Proto-Rabbinic traditions. The fact that the book of Daniel, very similar to that preserved in the Hebrew Bible, was accepted in all three religious centers creates a severe time problem for the critics. In the other two communities, a late date would mean that the book was almost certainly unknown before some of its prophecies were proven false.

Another problem arises at this point regarding the book's acceptance in Egypt or Babylon. Why would they care? It is almost a universal part of all works supporting the late date, that the book's acceptance relied heavily on its direct and integral application to the struggle of the Palestinian Jews. They were being oppressed by Antiochus, and their right to worship freely was being brutally extinguished. The book of Daniel addressed this and promised hope for the future. This is the reason, according to the book's critics, for Daniel's resonance and rapid recognition among the Palestinian Jews. How does this explain the books acceptance in Babylon and more particularly, Egypt? Not only did the prophetic chapters contain false prophecies, but they did not relate in any significant way with their daily lives or worship?

The suggestion that Daniel's acceptance has to do with the suspension of Temple sacrifice is equally difficult to support. There is no doubt that the desecration of the temple would have been widely published and lamented among Jews throughout the world. However, this would apply equally to the cleansing and resumption of activities there. The sacrifices resumed in 164 B.C., which would be at, or more probably before the time Daniel would have achieved any meaningful distribution in Palestine.

Factors affecting the book's acceptance would be different for the Diaspora Jews (those living outside of Palestine). The feelings and activities regarding temple worship and practices would have been relatively normal by exilic standards at the time the book had reached them. They would know about the temple's desecration, but also that it had been cleansed and the situation was now normal. In fact, almost all of the factors which militated for the book's acceptance in Palestine do not contribute very much at all to its acceptance elsewhere, especially in Egypt.

Despite the assertions for a late date, there is no reason why the book of Daniel would make any difference. The main reason suggested for its acceptance was immediately diminished by the success of the Maccabees and the restoration of the temple. Outside of Palestine, there was almost nothing which affected the daily worship of the exilic Jewish communities. I suggest, therefore, that the main reason proposed for the book's acceptance in the second-century B. C. is not as compelling as critics of Daniel would have us believe. In fact, there is every reason for supporters of the Book of Daniel to assert that the arguments of the critics are actually irrelevant, if not counter intuitive.

We have already illustrated that there are at least two textual traditions for Daniel, and suggested the likelihood of a third. The two we are sure of are the Proto-Massoretic (Palestine) and the LXX or Proto-LXX (Egypt) texts. At this point, the argument for a late date encounters another problem. The texts of Daniel at Qumran were of the Massoretic version of Daniel. According to Cross, the Massoretic, or more precisely Proto-Rabbinic, version is of Babylonian origin.

Some of the fragments of Daniel appear to be dated in the second-century B.C. The Qumran community began about 150 B.C., and certainly before 140 B.C., and there is a case for suggesting that Daniel was important to the community before it began. This means that the Massoretic text of Daniel is an exception to the rule regarding textual traditions, in that the book appears to have gone from Palestine to Babylon, then back to Palestine. Differences in the text indicate that during this time, the book was revised and rewritten. After being changed, these new revisions were accepted, and a different *vorlage* then made its way back to Palestine where it would have replaced the original textual tradition.

An associated problem with this scenario is that because of the incredibly short time involved, it is very likely that the author, scribes and those who assisted him in the creation and initial publication would now have begun to hear a different version of their own stories, which was in some ways distinct from that which they wrote and copied. This greatly reduces the likelihood that this revised, Proto-Massoretic version actually being accepted in Palestine and replacing the existing tradition.

The idea that the Proto-Massoretic (Proto-Rabbinic) was the original has its own, possibly greater problems. Most indications are that the LXX version which came from Egypt is actually older than the Massoretic textual tradition. Meadowcroft's observation deals specifically with the book of Daniel:

> Where there are significant differences between the texts, these are therefore likely to have arisen in the *Vorlage*. The considerable narrative differences that result must then be due in some measure to a less carefully crafted Semitic form of the stories. That in turn relates to the probability that the LXX *Vorlage* predates the form of Daniel 2-7 as preserved by the Masoretes.[77]

The texts at Qumran were not the only ones influenced by the LXX. According to the Anchor Bible Commentary:

Some phrases of LXX-Daniel appear in the Greek text of I Maccabees. From this evidence it can rightly be assumed that LXX-Daniel goes back to at least the date of the Greek text of I Maccabees. As I Maccabees, originally composed in Hebrew, was translated into Greek no earlier than 100 B.C., we may safely conclude that LXX_Daniel originated at about that time. It is generally agreed that LXX_Daniel was prepared in Egypt, presumably at Alexandria.[78]

While there is not enough information to create a perfect timetable of translations, revisions and recensions, the pattern is clear. The Septuagint text in Qumran "differs significantly from the Tiberian Massoretic text in some places."[79] Meadowcroft begins the Introduction to his book with the statement "One of the challenges of the book of Daniel is that the Septuagint (LXX) version of the book diverges from the Massoretic Text (MT) in significant ways."[80] It is also obvious that this divergence was substantial both in the number of differences, and the degree of variation found in them. The LXX and Massoretic texts represent truly different textual families.

Cross presents us with one of the essential factors for the development of textual families:

> The existence of textual families presumes some period of isolated development. When textual families come together they cross or conflate, or bring a textual crisis in which recensional activity occurs. At Qumran there is relatively little evidence of conflation or mixing, but there is some, on occasion recognizable in a marginal or interlinear addition of a later scribe.[81]

Isolation is essential to the development of the textual variation found in the different traditions of Bible texts. Cross mentions "some period of isolation" above, and he explains that this means a "required isolation over a considerable span of time."[82] I do not believe a period of thirty or forty years, even in the most extreme circumstances, would be given serious consideration as an explanation for the variations we find in Daniel.

We will return to our discussion regarding the importance of textual families, but first it will help us to discuss some of the more traditional linguistic questions directed at the early date theory. There are several standard linguistic objections to the early date composition of Daniel, but the most famous quote regarding the supposition of a late date comes from S.R. Driver:

> The verdict of the language of Daniel is thus clear. The *Persian* words presuppose a period after the Persian Empire had been well established: the Greek words *demand*, the Hebrew *supports*, and the Aramaic *permits*, a date after the conquest of Palestine by Alexander the Great (B.C. 332).[83]

This quote can be considered a "classic" in the critical analysis of Daniel, and is quoted or paraphrased in most works touching on this subject. It is echoed in the comments of scholars like Pfeiffer who wrote "The use of Persian and Greek (3:5, 15, etc.) words is likewise puzzling in the Neo-Babylonian periods."[84] Since most consider Daniel's use of these words as actual proof of a late date, and not must a mere 'puzzle', we will analyze Driver's statement by working backwards through its assertions.

First, that the date would be later than 332 B.C. If we accept that the book of Daniel must be dealt with as a unit, and not as individual parts, then this date itself precludes the acceptance of the late date of authorship. This would require the acceptance of the Hebrew part as truly prophetic in nature because of the accuracy in describing events in the third and second centuries B.C. However, I doubt that this was Driver's intention.

The Aramaic "permits" the imposition of a late date on the book of Daniel. This is not a very compelling statement, since implied in it is that it also "permits" us to accept the early date. Driver quietly attempts to identify the version of Aramaic used in Daniel as the "*Western* Aramaic dialect, of the type spoken in Palestine."[85] Others, however, have been less circumspect than Driver. The Abingdon Bible Commentary states "The language of the book, both Hebrew and the Aramaic, is of a much later date than the Exile."[86]

These arguments, however, are no longer valid. Further discoveries have rendered this argument obsolete. Philip R. Davies wrote:

> However, further discoveries of Aramaic texts, such as the Jewish archives from Elephantine in Egypt (early postexilic period) threw doubt upon the simplistic distinctions in vogue; and a development of fundamental importance was the identification of an Aramaic dialect which had been adopted officially by the Persian chancellery. It was dubbed 'Imperial Aramaic' or Official Aramaic, and it had been in use from the sixth century B.C. until the end of the third. [87]

The use of Imperial Aramaic is now generally accepted, but for some reason, appears to make no difference to the critics in the dating of Daniel.

One commentary simply confirms the use of Imperial Aramaic "which is dated roughly from 700 to 200 B.C. It seems best to place Daniel here even though the final written form of the book is dated somewhat later than 200 B.C."[88] This statement is somewhat problematic. This quote is from an entire volume dedicated to a study of the book of Daniel. To simply state that the prophetic section of the book was written near the middle of the second century, but that it was also written in a language that had disappeared long before that time, requires some explanation. None, however, is offered.

We can accept, therefore, that the Aramaic used in Daniel had spread over the entire region, "so that by the time of the Persian Empire (from 539 B.C.) it had become the international language of diplomacy, in itself, practically undatable with any conviction within c. 600 to 330 B.C'."[89]

The Aramaic, if suggesting any date at all, places the date of authorship well before the second century. It would also appear, then, that the Aramaic "problem" in Daniel is actually a problem for those proposing the second century as the period of authorship.

The Hebrew of Daniel does not really "support" anything about the date of authorship. There is no general agreement over just how much the Hebrew language changed during these centuries. If there is also no consensus on whether there were significant and identifiable changes to the language, it is difficult to suggest that these unidentified changes can be used for determining the time in which they book was written. Baldwin observes, "So far as the Hebrew is concerned there is little that can be proven concerning its date. Though, there must have been changes in Hebrew over the centuries, they are not easy to observe."[90]

What has been agreed upon by several experts is that the Hebrew of Daniel was not that of a native speaker. Cyrus Gordon comments on the contrast between the Hebrew and Aramaic, "The Aramaic is idiomatic and smooth; the Hebrew is artificial and inelegant, because the author knew Aramaic as a living language but Hebrew as a stilted dead language."[91] It is hard to understand how a Jewish scholar in Palestine would only know Hebrew as a dead language.

Davies interprets this a little differently than Gordon. He comments, "One may only comment that if the authors of the visions were scribes, as is widely believed, their standard of Hebrew is surprisingly poor."[92] The late date of authorship relies on the assumption that the book was written by an educated Jewish scholar, one well familiar with the sacred books and history, recent and ancient. The Hebrew employed, however, suggests that this was not the case. The Hebrew used may be considered more appropriate for a man who spoke Hebrew as a youth, but had Aramaic as his primary language for many years since.

Now we must decide if the Greek words do, indeed, *demand* that we accept a late date for Daniel. This idea, according to Yamauchi, "is based in part on the mistaken impression that it was only after the conquest of Alexander that there were widespread contacts with the Greeks in the Near East."[93] Such was not the case. As a result of excavations in Palestine, Harry Thomas Frank writes, "It is clear from them that Greek influence, popularly thought to have come with the conquests of Alexander the Great, was well established in Palestine in the centuries prior to the coming of his armies and the settlement of his veterans on the soil."[94]

There are many other examples of Greek influence in the Near East. We will recall that the battle of Carchemish occurred before Nebuchadnezzar became king. Excavations of that battle field find that Greek mercenaries were actually involved, fighting with *both* sides, Egyptian and Babylonian.[95] With the mounting evidence of Greek contact at an early date, many no longer make a point regarding Daniel's use of Greek words as significant.

We should, nevertheless, at least discuss these Greek words. There are only three of them, and they all refer to musical instruments. Alfred Sendry, in his book

Music in Ancient Israel[96], suggests that one of them was not actually a Greek instrument at all, but actually been imported by the Greeks from the east. Another was mistranslated, because the ancient meaning, implied by Daniel, was misunderstood by the later translator.

The Babylonians and Persians both had extensive contacts with the Ionian Greeks as well. The fact that a few examples of their musical instruments are found further east is not at all unexpected. What may have been more singular, is that there were not more such words. Baldwin comments, "What is significant is that there are so few Greek loanwords in the Aramaic of Daniel."[97] This is especially valid if the book had been written during the second century B.C., when Greek was becoming the common, daily language of the region.

One group of words briefly mentioned by Driver was Daniel's use of Persian words. One comment regarding their occurrence in Daniel should prove interesting. Baldwin presents the following regarding these Persian words based on the work of K.A. Kitchen:

> There are six terms [Persian words] that have not so far been found to occur after c. 330 BC, and certain terms were not understood by the Old Greek translators. He makes one further point, namely that the Persian words in Daniel are *Old Persian words*, that is belonging to the period before c. 300 BC. The evidence is thus in favor of an earlier rather than a later date, and Kitchen concludes (p, 77)"
> "These facts suggest an origin for the Persian words in the Aramaic of Daniel before c. 300 BC.' (Kitchen, "Notes on Some Problems", 35-44)[98]

Driver's insistence that linguistic evidence proves the

late date is no longer as powerful in light of these further discoveries. In fact, as we have demonstrated, the evidence may now favor the opposite conclusion and give more credence to the arguments for an early date of authorship. Meadowcroft observes in his study on the language of Daniel:

> I have paid little attention to the linguistic evidence for dating the Aramaic of the MT. However, a number of studies have recently cast doubt on Driver's famous assertion that 'the Greek words demand, the Hebrew supports, and the Aramaic permits, a date after the conquest of Palestine by Alexander the Great (BC 332)'. Kitchen took issue with Driver in 1965 when he demonstrated a number of linguistic features that could indicate an earlier date for the stories. Although Kitchen himself has not returned to that particular fray since, others have accumulated more evidence that supports his thesis.[99]

While our understanding of the ancient Near East has grown, this improved understanding has often been ignored by Daniel's critics. After examining the progress made in the study of the texts of Daniel and then reviewing the criticism of it, we again get the impression that there is a late date bias regarding the linguistic analysis. The occurrence of three Greek musical instruments sparked almost universal support for the idea of a late date. Yet our examination of the time required for the book to have been written, reproduced, distributed, accepted and translated demands a schedule that would be difficult to meet mere decades ago. The successful process demanded by those suggesting a late date of authorship would seemingly require computerized publication and overnight delivery. Even with this in mind, the significant time problem associated with a second-century B.C. composition is met with a superficial analysis amounting to "It doesn't seem right, but I'm sure there's a good reason."

There are several topics dealing with the Daniel in a second-century B.C. context that have not been explored. One is the now recognized importance of Daniel in the Qumran community. It is possible that the community was founded as early as 150 B.C., and it is suggested that those founding Qumran had already developed a strong affinity for Daniel. *The Anchor Bible Reference* observes:

> It is difficult to define precisely the role of another leadership type, the "maskil." The word itself derives from a verb, meaning "to enlighten," and it might be translated literally as "enlightener," that is, "instructor." No doubt the use of the term was influenced by Daniel 12 -- a chapter known to have been influential in Qumran sectarian texts -- in which the term appears twice (verses 3 and 10).[100]

The important community texts, Testament of Levi"[101] and "The New Jerusalem,"[102] both contain sections which are based on Daniel.

There are some who suggest that the Septuagint translation of Deuteronomy 32:8 is based on the tenth chapter of Daniel. The idea of guardian angels having control of districts, which is presented there, seems to have originated with Daniel. The date of translation for Deuteronomy is about one-hundred years prior to the late date for Daniel.

It also appears that the standard of analysis applied to other biblical texts is not deemed valid for the dating of Daniel. The dating of some of the Psalms, for example, was pushed back several hundred years based on their presence at Qumran. William Brownlee wrote about Old Testament canon this way:

> It would seem that we should abandon the idea of any of the canonical psalms being of Maccabean date, for each song had to win its way in the esteem of the people before it could be included in the sacred compilation of the Psalter. Immediate entrée for any of them is highly improbable.[103]

If immediate acceptance is highly improbable for a Scriptural Text, in this case a Psalm, why isn't this standard applied to Daniel? Again, this rule applies to all the books in the Bible except Daniel.

Even Frank Cross displays an obvious double standard with regards to Daniel. This section will be a bit long, but it will demonstrate the process that would normally be applied to textual analysis. This is Cross' argument when alternate theories are put forward regarding the origin of textual families:

> Thus we propose three local texts, and assign them with descending levels of confidence to Palestine, Egypt, and Babylonia. Alternate theories can and have been proposed. It has been suggested that different parties or sects within Palestinian Judaism may have provided isolated contexts in which the several textual families developed. It might be argued that Zadokites of Samaria, Qumran and the Temple used predominantly texts I have called Palestinian, the Pharisees the proto-Rabbinic type, the Hellenistic party the Hebrew texts underlying the Greek Pentateuch. Such a proposal labors, I

think, against insurmountable difficulties. The party divisions are relatively late and give insufficient time for the slow process of evolution, largely produced by inadvertent copyists' errors, which gave rise to distinct textual families. The Jewish sects crystallized in the Hasmonaean period, in the second century B.C. Nor does it appear plausible that two or three text types could live alongside one another in Jerusalem for centuries even in different sociological or religious groups without mixing. Finally, one is struck with the fact that Palestinian Jewish works such as Jubilees (pre-Essene), Josephus' Antiquities, Pseudo-Philo's *Liber antiquitatum biblicarum* (written in Hebrew no later than 70 C.E.) all reflect the Palestinian Hebrew text type, not the proto-Rabbinic, in biblical quotations.[104]

The phrase "The party divisions are relatively late and give insufficient time for the slow process of evolution" is correct. However, their application is apparently not universal, since it is not used in the analysis of Daniel.

The process of acceptance into canon is long and difficult – except for Daniel. The Proto-Rabbinical texts are usually from Babylonian origin – except for Daniel. Biblical books whose texts were found at Qumran are assumed to be hundreds of years old – except Daniel. After studying the criticism of Daniel, I have arrived at my "Except it or Accept it" process of analysis. They are force to either "except" Daniel from the standard rules of textual dating, as shown above, or be forced to "accept" it as a work originating from the Babylonian exile, which they are unwilling to do.

The Anchor Bible Commentary continues this

trend:

> Whatever the merits of the case presented by Cross with regard to the older books of the Hebrew Bible that may have had such a complex textual history, his theory of local texts would not apply to the Book of Daniel. The reason is that, as Cross himself writes, "distinct textual families take centuries to develop," and the MT - form of Daniel is simply not old enough to develop into three textual traditions.[105]

Yet, three textual traditions for Daniel do exist. This is another example where an open and impartial analysis would be very revealing, but is not being done because the answers have already been decided.

Section 6: Conclusion

We have endeavored to provide sufficient analysis to answer this question: How valid are the arguments which form the basis for the dating of the book of Daniel as a second-century work? This chapter has presented the major arguments related to the dating and authorship of Daniel. Unfortunately, the main questions remain unanswered. Ongoing study and discovery will undoubtedly cause opinions to fluctuate, but a final answer may never be found. In the meantime, the weight of evidence will swing from favoring one side of the discussion to the other and back, and most opinions will ultimately remain unchanged.

The core issue of Daniel revolves around its status as a book of prophecy, which makes it a question of faith not scholarly analysis. If one accepts that God exists, that He does speak to men and that the Bible is a collection of these pronouncements, then the prophecies of Daniel are easily accepted. If the Bible is simply one of many "Wisdom Books," an alternate explanation must be found for its writings.

The first section of this thesis suggested that the book of Daniel must be dealt with as a unit and not as individual sections. There are many factors which support this conclusion. There is an identifiable structure to the book, which extends from the first chapter to the last. Many scholars suggest there was a specific literary form, the chiasm, used in the book as a whole, and individual sections of the book.

The style and theme of the book are also consistent throughout. Even though the language changes from Hebrew to Aramaic and back, specific characteristics suggest that the same author wrote them all. The amount of evidence suggesting there was but a single author is so great, that most critics have conceded this point.

The second section dealt with specific questions regarding events recorded in Daniel. The accepted academic position has been that all historical and scientific information concerning the book concur with the late date theory. Again, we must recall Cyrus Gordon's assertion of "grotesque errors' in Daniel.

This section addressed a number of specific historical questions. The first verse is assailed for several reasons. We showed that the questions regarding the date of the battle at Carchemish have several possible explanations. The dating from Jeremiah differs from Daniel's, but this what we would expect. Jeremiah in Israel was a prophet while Daniel was an administrator from Babylon. Daniel's date would be correct by either of the administrative calendars, from Judah or Babylon.

The doubts about the capture of Jerusalem at this time have also been addressed. The situation after the battle of Carchemish offers very little room for criticism. The Egyptian army was in full flight, and was pursued by Nebuchadnezzar and the Babylonian army to the border of Egypt. This would have taken the Babylonian army past Jerusalem. Under these circumstances, we would expect a force would be sent to Jehoiakim to either secure his fealty or contain his forces until they could be dealt with properly.

All of the questions regarding the first verse of Daniel have answers. These answers, while not offering conclusive proof for or against a particular date of authorship, offer no real problem for those who hold to a sixth-century date.

The term "Chaldean" is also considered a significant indication of a late date of composition. However, no actual examples have been given which substantiate this claim. Those who have attempted to analyze the usage of the term "Chaldean" during in a Neo-Babylonian context have been unable to find examples upon which to base an analysis.

Until the appearance of a comprehensive study which shows that the term was not used with the same meaning as Daniel, it must be considered a supposition at best. A point of irony may be in order here. If no examples from the ancient texts can be found, Daniel itself may be the only proof they have that the term Chaldean was used in a racial context, as it is on at least two occasions. There is something very wrong with an argument based, even in part, on the reliability of the book it is attempting to refute.

On the contrary, there is some support for Daniel's use of the name. We know that much of the book was written during the Persian period, and the writings of Herodotus, about half a century later, do mention the Chaldeans and provide a meaning. The Chaldeans officiated for the gods, and acted as intermediaries. This corresponds very well with Daniel's usage, and indicates that the book may be more accurate than its critics.

The interpretation of Nebuchadnezzar's first dream provides a situation in which the critics are forced into an argument that they don't all agree with.

The fourth section of the statue was almost universally understood to be Rome until the book began to be the subject of historical rather than prophetic interpretation. Since Rome did not fulfill the prophecy until much later than the book's writing, it had to be disqualified as a possible candidate for this last kingdom.

Rome was replaced by Greece, but this left no kingdom to fill the second position. The only possible candidate for the second kingdom was that of the Medes, even though it does not fill the requirements. Many critics acknowledge that the Median Empire is not correct. We are left with the reality that the prophetic sequence of Daniel is superior to the historically imposed alternative presented by its critics.

Questions about the period of Nebuchadnezzar's madness are a very weak at best. There is no information from that period which would support or discredit the account of Daniel. While there is a document from Qumran that indicates some parallels with Nabonidus, there is no solid basis for asserting its accuracy. On the other hand, there seems to be historical evidence that confirms some of the events recorded in Daniel.

Events in the fifth chapter of Daniel have also been attacked as inaccurate. However, the instances regarding Daniel's references to Belshazzar as Nebuchadnezzar's son have been shown to be accurate. The term "father," used in this context, is perfectly acceptable when referring to one's grandfather, and it is understandable that Belshazzar would have preferred the association with Babylon's greatest king, instead of to the madman many considered his father to be.

The identity of Darius the Mede is still unresolved. There is no denying that this name is totally unknown in the history of that time. Critics have a number of explanations for this, from "The author made it up" to "The author had him confused with Darius I who came later." We may assert, however, that these arguments are actually contradicted by the very premise upon which their whole theory is based. While they assert that the book is the work of a skilled, highly educated Jew of the second-century B.C., they are forced to contradict this by asserting that he was unfamiliar with many obvious and well known facts of history. I believe that mention of Darius the Mede actually strengthens the credibility of the author. I have a difficult time believing that the reference was made in error.

Critics ask why there is no mention of such a famous person such as Daniel outside of the book itself. Ben Sira omits Daniel, but also overlooks several others, including a surprisingly large percentage of Daniel's prominent contemporaries. The fact that four important Israelites from this time, with books of scripture bearing their names, were overlooked suggests that other factors are at work. This omission probably has nothing to do with the existence of Daniel himself.

Ezekiel does mention a Daniel, but there are questions whether this refers to the Daniel we are discussing. The argument that the "Daniel" mentioned in Ezekiel is the "Danel" from Canaanite literature does not bear close scrutiny. The pagan king Danel exemplified the very characteristics which Ezekiel was speaking against, and it is very difficult to accept that a favorite of the god Bel would be compared to Noah. On the other hand, the fame of Daniel and his four friends and associates would have spread throughout the Jewish world and his success while staying true to his religion would have been a powerful example of faithfulness.

The fact that Daniel was included in the Writings portion of the Hebrew scripture makes perfect sense. Daniel was not a prophet in the traditional sense, and much of his writings were directed to the gentile nations. There is almost no communication of God's will to his people, which was considered the major work of a prophet. The "Writings" contained the historical books, and this was the appropriate place for Daniel.

It should be understood, however, that Daniel enjoyed the status of prophet among the people. The writings of Qumran, the New Testament, and the writings of the historian Josephus all explicitly refer to Daniel as a prophet, and give his writings equal weight with any of the other prophets. Josephus, in the first-century A.D. refers to Daniel as one of the greatest prophets in Jewish history.

Linguistically, there are several facts that must be addressed. In the opinion of many scholars, the language of Daniel contains many characteristics which strongly suggest its composition occurred before 300 B.C., well before the prophetic sections were fulfilled. The Aramaic language used, and many of the Persian words employed in the Book of Daniel, cast serious doubts on a late date of authorship, while at the same time they are perfectly compatible with the sixth-century date. Greek words, once considered proof positive of its late date of authorship, are now perfectly compatible with the sixth-century B.C. time frame. In fact, the very limited and specialized occurrence of Greek words argues against it being composed hundreds of years after Greek became such a common language throughout the land.

The process by which a book gained acceptance as scripture was examined. It normally took hundreds of years for a book to be accepted, and many more to then be carried to the other centers of Jewish culture. Even more years are required for it to develop a separate textual tradition in these new centers. Some of the Psalms, once thought to be of Maccabean date, had their estimated date of origin pushed back almost two hundred years because a copy was found in the Dead Sea Scrolls. This was not the case with Daniel, even though Daniel played a significant role in the beliefs and organization of the Qumran Community.

Considering the significantly different textual

traditions and its inclusion as an important text in Qumran, it is extremely difficult to accept Daniel as a product of the second-century B.C. All of the main textual traditions of scripture include portions of the specific verses that are considered proof that the book was written no earlier than 167 B.C., yet none of these traditions could possibly have developed within the time this date would require. The numbers are virtually impossible to reconcile.

Add to this that the supposedly new book of Daniel would contradict accepted scripture, and would contain what the critics consider to be verifiably false prophecies, and the case for acceptance of a late date composition gets weaker. In Egypt and Babylon, there would be no real national or religious need for the writings of Daniel. The persecutions of the Palestinian Jews would have been stories, which had resolved themselves and returned to normal by the time the Exiled Jews received their first exposure to the book. Despite all of these problems, Daniel was accepted as prophecy and included in all versions of scripture. It is very difficult to support the idea that a text which what would certainly be recognized as a contemporary, and contained historical errors, could be immediately accepted under these circumstances.

Section 7: Final Observations

After spending hundreds of hours in research and evaluation, there are some general impressions that I think may be of interest to the reader. They do not fit the criteria for academic consideration, but still reflect directly on the topic. These final observations are personal, and no attempt will be made to document or support them. They are presented with the hope that they may engender some further consideration on the part of the reader.

First, I think it is quite misleading to portray this debate as a battle between two theories of authorship, as I have found only one theory. Those supporting the early date of authorship of Daniel almost universally assert that Daniel was not only the principal character, also its author. There are many facts corroborating Daniel as author, facts which explain many of the details surrounding the book's purpose and origin.

Those supporting a late date have few commonly held theories, and an almost total absence of factual evidence upon which to base them. The two arguments common among all of the books critics are that it was completed between 167 and 165 B.C., and that Daniel himself couldn't have written it. Beyond that, disagreements between the critics themselves are as great as with the supporters of the book.

The points of disagreement among the critics occur on some very fundamental points. They do not agree on how many authors there were. They cannot decide what language it was written in. They disagree over the interpretation of some of the revelations and prophecies. They cannot even agree on the question of whether Daniel was a real person or simply a myth. The two criticisms of the book presented above are all that links many of these critics and their opinions.

Proponents of a late date have absolutely no ideas regarding Daniel's authorship. They suspect that he was a Jew, but disagree on whether he was highly educated and meticulous, or sloppy and ignorant of the basic facts of history. With all of their study, examination and theorizing, none have ever suggested an alternative author. They have no idea who wrote the book.

They don't really know where it was written, either. Studies of the version of Daniel from the Hebrew scripture suggest it may have been written in Babylon, while an examination of the Septuagint gives the impression that this Greek version originated in Palestine. The best they can say is that he was probably a Jew from somewhere. This isn't even a well-formed idea, much less an actual theory on authorship. Until there is some real indication in a late date context of who wrote the book and where, it is very difficult to suggest that an alternate theory of authorship to the traditional one which actually exists. The only true theory of authorship is that the book was originally written by Daniel near the end of his life. As just stated, many disagree with this but offer no real alternative.

    The preceding situation created another problem. The late date has been so firmly and completely accepted in academic circles, that it became the only possible conclusion for any evaluation. Since they already knew the answer, they merely had to determine how any new information fit into that framework.

    This approach to scholarship is not completely honest. If all of the facts were impartially evaluated, free from this predetermined dating theory, I believe that different conclusions would have been reached regarding Daniel. Also, I suspect that most critics would be forced to reclassify the disputed passages from the book. While they may not prove an early date, they no longer support the late date authorship.

    As mentioned previously, it appears that most of the doubts about Daniel emanate from a central core of rejection, the rejection of prophecy as a possible origin of the book. It is true that knowledge received by revelation does not allow for the usual evaluation based on the rules of science, but that does not make them false. It's a mistake to limit man's universe by excluding things we don't understand or can't measure.

    As I evaluated many of the arguments against the book of Daniel, my mind kept returning to chapter two of the book. Daniel himself seems to anticipate these objections:

The Chaldeans answered before the king, and said, There is not a man

> **upon the earth that can shew the king's matter: therefore there is no king, Lord, nor ruler, that asked such things at any magician, or astrologer, or Chaldean. And it is a rare thing that the king requireth, and there is none other that can shew it before the king, except the gods, whose dwelling is not with flesh. (Daniel 2: 10, 11)**

The Chaldeans were only able to deal with what they could hear, see or touch. These same limitations exist today, as scholars are limited by what they can observe, measure and verify. Centuries ago, however, Daniel was able to prove that there is a power beyond human understanding, which can give knowledge and wisdom to men.

Scientific discoveries over the past century have shown that the stories of Daniel are increasingly accurate. Imagine the irony if archaeologists finally do find the missing keys to proving the veracity of Daniel, and by doing so prove the true prophetic nature of its stories. The revelations previously rejected by these scholars would then be the means for silencing a new set of skeptics thousands of years into Daniel's future. While scientific proof is not necessary where faith exists, truth will ultimately be validated.

My opinion is that Daniel has yet to receive a proper evaluation based on current scholarship. I fear that currently, many of the most capable scholars on Daniel have never taken an entirely impartial look at the subject. I believe that more evidence supporting the account in Daniel would be found if these experts could begin their analysis again, but without any preformed ideas.

My last opinion may come as a surprise, considering the material and opinions I have presented to this point. I do not believe that the book of Daniel, as found in modern English and Hebrew scripture, was necessisarily written by the prophet Daniel in the sixth-century B.C., in the exact for found in the modern Christian Bible. Modern and ancient scripture themselves do not agree on the exact wording and sequence of Daniel. The essential elements are present in all the different versions, but the different translations and versions at times vary greatly.

It is very difficult to believe that a book passed through the centuries without some modification. That said, I do believe the prophecies and revelations contained in the book did originate with that prophet. The skepticism of the critics invariably begins with the rejection of prophecy as a possible explanation for the accuracy of the book's content. However, I contend that prophecy is an essential part of Daniel, and all other scripture. I have come to believe that Daniel did write these prophecies, and they were preserved and passed to later generations. They were not necessarily written as polished literary works but as simple descriptions of God's efforts and plans for His children.

As was noted in the text, the original Septuagint contains the same revelations and teachings and the Hebrew texts, but their organization and presentation are less sophisticated and stylish. Some may suggest that this raises questions as to the reliability of Daniel. How reliable is the final Hebrew version if it varies from the earlier texts?

I have no issue with the presentation of Daniel being tailored for a specific audience. In the same way, I would have no problem letting my son or daughter read a Bible version in simplified language for children. And, while I read the King James Version, I would have no issue with anyone preferring a version written in contemporary English if it helped them understand the message and spirit of God's Word. None of us read the original text, all versions have been transmitted to us with changes – translation itself is a change.

I believe that one of the factors for the selection of the current textual version was the beauty of its form. I have read or recited the Lord's Prayer hundreds, if not thousands of times. It is a beautiful expression of man's reliance and devotion to God. Yet no reading will ever have the impact on my soul which I get from hearing a beautifully performed musical rendition of the same verses. The creative power of the art of music has a way of carrying this scripture directly past the mind and into the heart of those hearing it. I believe this is what the Hebrew form of Daniel is.

The teachings of Daniel, for me, are the work of a sixth-century prophet named Daniel. If, however, they were creatively presented by the touch of an artist – literary in this case instead of musical – I have no problem with the result. In fact, I find the current version inspiring, no matter which Bible version it may be read from.

CHAPTER 4

Section 1: Review

The purpose of this thesis was to examine questions relating to the dating and authorship of the book of Daniel. The traditional view asserts that the book was completed in the second-century B.C., and was not composed by Daniel whose name the book carries. This would then exclude the possibility of the book of Daniel being a prophetic work and instead placing it the category of historical fiction.

The study above examined the various arguments which suggest the second-century date with the following objectives:

> 1) To provide an overview of the significant areas of disagreement regarding the book of Daniel, and what facts form the basis for this disagreement.
>
> 2) How are the facts interpreted to support one opinion over the other, or alternately used to counter those arguments.
>
> 3) To demonstrate that there has been an expansion of relevant data regarding the book of Daniel. This data is found generally in the areas

of historical and linguistic research.

4) To determine the effect of the data, especially that which is newly introduced into the discussion, on the final conclusions regarding the date and authorship of the book Daniel.

A study was made of all available material relating directly or indirectly to the subject. This debate began almost two thousand years ago, and while the details of it have changed the basic assertions have not. The traditional, almost universally accepted view which continued from before Christ until the last century held that Daniel himself wrote the book in the late sixth-century B.C. The modern view asserts that it was written sometime in the second-century B.C.

The debate usually revolves around three areas of study. First, the book relates details of historical people and events whose authenticity is challenged. Second, the book makes indirect references which some suggest demonstrates a context other than that suggested by the book itself. Third, some assert that the language of the book is not that of the sixth-century B.C., and instead supports the later date of authorship.

The study began with the very first verse of Daniel, and progressed through the book and presenting the questions as they were encountered. The questions were first introduced and the problems asserted by the critics were then discussed. The opposing views were also presented and discussed, and a conclusion was sometimes presented.

Section 2: Discussion

Our analysis of the first purpose listed above dealt with the important points of disagreement. It accomplished this by introducing the questions, which according to its critics, cast doubt on the authenticity of the book of Daniel as a prophetic work. These questions were then analyzed for accuracy and relevance to the discussion. We also dealt with those factors critics present as proof of a second-century authorship.

There are a number of historical and linguistic questions which arise from a study of Daniel. It was the goal of this work to determine whether the events in question are presented accurately in the text, or whether the critics are correct in their skepticism. If it was determined that events or individuals are portrayed incorrectly, then we will have had little choice but to give careful consideration the questions being suggested relating to Daniel's authenticity.

There can be no disagreement on the part of those who support the traditional view of Daniel, on the need to examine these questions. If we are confident that the book of Daniel is indeed a prophetic book, written by Daniel during his time in Babylon, then we must be equally confident that an analysis of facts will ultimately demonstrate this to be true. Any new or additional information will only serve to broaden and enhance our understanding of the book.

The second purpose was to determine how these facts actually affected our analysis of the book. As each question was discussed, and the information related to that specific issue examined, we had to ultimately determine its impact. Many of the facts used to criticize the authenticity of Daniel did not hold up under careful examination. As mentioned early in this paper, some of the most important criticism of the book may now actually be interpreted as supporting it.

The use of Greek words in Daniel, according to almost every critic, "demands" that the book be dated after the third century B.C. However, when we examined the circumstances which may have contributed to the use of these words, the situation changed. The possibility of Greek influence, especially in the area of music, is entirely possible - if not actually probable. In rebuttal to the critics, we should probably expect that Daniel would exhibit more Greek influence if the book were actually written after two hundred years under Greek domination. The three words of Greek in Daniel can be therefore be used as arguments for both sides of the question.

The third objective related to the expansion of relevant data on the book. We presented several instances where ongoing discoveries have added to the body of material relating to our discussion. The Dead Sea Scrolls have been, and will continue to be, an important source of information. They not only help us understand the content of the book, but also help us understand the way it was thought of at a critical point in history.

The texts from Elephantine in Egypt, contracts from Babylon spanning the time of the Neo-Babylonian empire to Persian conquest, and temple ruins from Harran all have provided important information about the period. There will certainly be more information forthcoming, and we should be excited at the prospect. Again, if we are confident that the book of Daniel is indeed a prophetic book, written by Daniel during his time in Babylon, then we must be equally confident that additional information will ultimately support this.

The fourth and final objective was to determine the effect of the new data on our conclusions regarding the book. The recently discovered Aramaic documents from Elephantine, just mentioned, had a dramatic effect on the linguistic arguments regarding Daniel. The critics have always suggested that the Aramaic dialect used in Daniel was not indicative of the common language in use at the time the book was supposed to have been written. This was once believed to be true, but we now have more examples of the language's use, and opinions have changed.

The existence of "Imperial or Official Aramaic," which disappeared before the suggested late date of authorship, was established by new discoveries. What once suggested the accuracy of the critics position, may now be interpreted to support the traditional, early date opinion. Ongoing research and excavation have indeed changed the discussion, and will continue to do so.

Another goal of this analysis was to determine the validity the questions presented. Not all of the questions are of equal importance. Many of them would not have been raised at all in the absence of the other, more significant issues.

As an example, the reference to Nebuchadnezzar as "king" at the beginning of Daniel is often questioned, since he was actually crown-prince at that time. Some critics present this argument, but I considered it too weak for consideration. It is true that Nebuchadnezzar was not king when these events transpired, but it still fits within common usage of the title. If we read a biography of Ronald Reagan, and found a picture with this caption, "This is the high school that President Clinton graduated from," it would not be criticized - the caption would not be considered an error. It is true that Bill Clinton was not president while he attended the school, "President Clinton" was never a student there. However, "President Clinton" is the name by which he is currently best known. Daniel, also, would have never known Nebuchadnezzar by any other title than "King." This brief example shows that not all arguments are equally valid.

This question has little value in our discussion, and would probably have never been suggested in the absence more substantial issues. The question of why Daniel referred to these events happening in the third year of Jehoiakim, on the other hand, is very valid. There is no obvious explanation of why Daniel would have used a different date from other scriptural references. This question demands an explanation.

Section 3 - Interpretation

In the writer's opinion, the data presented does not provide us with a definitive response to our fundamental question. The goal of this thesis was to examine the validity of the suggested proofs for a second-century authorship of the Book of Daniel. This paper examined the most common and compelling issues, presenting both sides of each issue, and an evaluation of the competing interpretations. However, the question of validity is not easily answered. There is no doubt that many of the questions regarding Daniel are valid, and still have no definitive answer. We are unable, for example, to positively identify the historical character of Darius the Mede. Therefore, asking critical question on the subject is perfectly valid and necessary.

There is another aspect to our question of validity. The legitimacy of a question regarding the date of authorship is not proof that one theory of dating is correct or incorrect. Referring again to Darius the Mede, while it is perfectly acceptable to question his identity, it is not acceptable to claim that the question itself decides the controversy. The arguments may support one theory, but none of them are conclusive. Also, there exists a valid candidate for Darius in history, Cyrus the Great. The fact that there are valid candidates does not prove the late-date, the fact that there are questions does not disprove it.

This is the situation with all of the questions raised by the book's critics. We were unable to find any indisputable questions regarding the authenticity of Daniel. Every difficulty or question challenging the existence of a prophet named Daniel as the book's author, has equally acceptable answers supporting that claim. None of the questions raised are able to firmly establish a second-century date of origin for the book.

Restating the conclusion, while few of these questions are definitively resolved, they all have acceptable alternatives. The date for Nebuchadnezzar's first capture of Jerusalem varies between Daniel and other scriptures, but this is perfectly acceptable when one takes into account the different calendars used by the different writers. The question is valid but so are the explanations.

The same process works in reverse. The fact that Babylon fell to the Persians during a feast is corroborated by independent historical references, but it is possible that these references could have been available to the author. The facts seem to suggest that Daniels is indeed correct, but there are other explanations that do not necessary make it an eye-witness account.

However, critics do not have satisfactory answers to some of the arguments suggested by the book's supporters. How did the author of Daniel know the name Belshazzar, and that he was acting as regent in Babylon before its fall to Cyrus? The name of Belshazzar was completely forgotten, except in Daniel, until recent discoveries reintroduced it. How did the author of Daniel know that it was Nebuchadnezzar who rebuilt Babylon? While modern research has indeed confirmed this, there is no indication whatsoever that anyone alive during the second-century B.C. had this information. The assertion that "there must have been something that provided this information" is simply not enough.

Finally, I believe the most compelling argument in the entire debate supports an early date of authorship. The time required for a book to receive canonization and universal acceptance is well documented, and measured in centuries. If critics cannot offer justification as to why Daniel must be excepted from the normal process and requirement for acceptance as scripture, then they cannot be surprised when millions of Christians around the world accept the book as scripture. When one accepts that the prophetic nature of Daniel is confirmed, it stands as a powerful witness for the prophet role of the Bible as a whole.

So, I repeat the question: "If Daniel did not write the book, then who did?" The period in which the book was supposed to have been written is now fairly rich in historical detail. The Dead Seas Scrolls, the writings of Josephus, the Bible and other writings all originated near this time. All indications are that Daniel was well-known and highly respected, yet there is absolutely no indication that anyone alive at that time believed the book had any author other than Daniel. None give a hint that Daniel was a recent composition. The critics have no positive support or proof of their position.

While disagreements over the authenticity of Daniel still exist, and will certainly continue well into the future, the argument is no longer one sided. Recent discoveries and analysis seem to be moving the debate in favor of the traditional, sixth-century date of authorship. Those who have made a decision on the truth of Daniel based on faith are now being vindicated. However, for those who have made a decision on the truth of Daniel based on faith, no vindication is necessary.

APPENDIX A

Detailed Historical Outline

This is a more detailed history of the region, and gives additional information about the rulers and political dynamics during this critical period of history. The more comprehensive our understand about this period, the greater our appreciation of the Book of Daniel itself.

Immediately preceding the resurgence of Babylon, the Assyrians ruled their empire from Nineveh. In 627 B.C., the Assyrian empire was weakened by revolts following the death of King Ashurbanipal. This eventually led to attacks from a coalition of Babylonian and Median forces in 612 B.C. After the fall of the city of Nineveh to the Babylonians and Medians, Assyrian forces moved to Harran where they continued to fight the Babylonians. Their leader, Assur-uballit was successful in enlisting the aid of the Egyptians, but still lost control of the new capital of Harran and was forced to retreat west across the Euphrates River.

In 609 B.C. Josiah, king of Judah, attempted to assist the Babylonians by preventing Egyptian troops from reaching their Assyrian allies. He was defeated and killed by Pharaoh Necho, who placed Jehoiakim on the throne. The Egyptians were then able to join forces with the Assyrians, but they were still unable to maintain control over Harran.

In 605 B.C. the Egyptians, and what was left of the Assyrian forces, made a stand near the city of Carchemish. The Babylonians, under the command of crown-prince Nebuchadnezzar, crossed the Euphrates River and defeated the Egyptians decisively. The Babylonians pursued the fleeing Egyptians in hopes of completely destroying the Egyptian army. Nebuchadnezzar and his army chased them to the Egyptians border. At this point, however, King Nabopolassar died in Babylon, and Nebuchadnezzar had to hurry back to Babylon to assume the duties of king. He was able, however, to assert control over the lands of Syria and Palestine before returning.

Over the next several years, Nebuchadnezzar found it necessary to return to Syria and Palestine to counter Egyptian attempts to reassert their influence there. Nebuchadnezzar was finally forced to capture Jerusalem again, and in 597 B.C. he took Jehoiachin, Jehoiakim's son, and a large portion of the nation into captivity in Babylon. The Jews revolted again in 588 B.C. and Nebuchadnezzar responded forcefully. Most of the remaining Jews were also taken to Babylon, while many others fled to Egypt for safety.

Nebuchadnezzar was a capable and energetic king, and was active both at home and abroad. He was responsible for extensive building and beautification projects in Babylon and other major cities, as well as expanding the size of his empire. He conducted a 13-year siege of Tyre on the Mediterranean coast of Syria, and even invaded Egypt in 568 B.C.

Nebuchadnezzar's military and economic success brought an extended period of prosperity and peace to the land of Babylon. His success also inspired a religious revival, and he became very active in building and refurbishing a number of the temples in the land. This is the time when historians claim that

Nebuchadnezzar created the Hanging Gardens of Babylon, one of the Seven Wonders of the World, so his Median wife Amyitis would feel more at home.

In October of 562 Nebuchadnezzar died, and was replaced by his son Amel-Marduk (know as Evil-Merodach in the Bible). It is believed that Amel-Marduk ruled in an erratic and reckless manner. It is commonly held that Amel-Marduk did release Jehoiachin from prison and allowed him a seat at the royal table. Amel-Marduk was eventually murdered by his brother-in-law Neriglissar (Nergal-shar-usur) in 560 B.C.

Neriglissar ruled from 560-556 B.C. He had minor military successes, but also had to face economic problems at home. He died in 556 and was replaced by his young son, Larbashi-Marduk. Larbashi-Marduk displayed such a propensity for evil, that he was quickly assassinated.

Nabonidus (Nabu Na'id) next became king. The son of a nobleman named Nabu-balatsu-iqbi, his mother was a priestess of the moon god Sin (called Nanna by the Sumerians). It is suggested that his mother's name was Adda-Goppi. Nabonidus married Nebuchadnezzar's daughter, Nitocris, which made him more acceptable to the priests and businessmen of Babylon who supported his ascension. Nabonidus was a huge disappointment to all.

Nabonidus was almost as devoted to the god Sin as to his mother. Marduk, however, was the god of Babylon, and the king had such a conflict with the priests of Marduk that he went into self-imposed exile for ten years. During this period, the New Year festival was not observed, with severe religious and economic repercussions. Nabonidus received the nickname of the 'Royal Archaeologist' because of his interest in the past and excavations of historical sites.

During the absence of Nabonidus, his son Belshazzar assumed most of the administrative duties regarding the capital. He was named co-regent in about

554 B.C., but was not a skilled administrator or governor. The existing economic problems in Babylon, caused by the religious problems and neglected celebrations as previously mentioned, worsened. In 539 B.C., an army of Persians and Medians captured Babylon and ended the rule of the Chaldean kings.

Cyrus became the first ruler of the Persian Empire, and was responsible for the final destruction of the Neo-Babylonian Empire. He was born about 600 B.C., the son of the Persian King Cambyses and Mandane, daughter of the Median king Astyages. The Medes and the Persians were closely related cultures, both speaking similar languages and living in what is today part of northern Iran.

The Medes were initially the dominant group, both militarily and culturally. They created an Empire which included the Persians, and eventually a part of the Assyrian Empire which they had helped to destroy. Even though they were closely related, the Medians considered the Persians as a vassal state, demanding annual tribute.

In about 558 B.C., Cyrus became ruler of the Persian kingdom, and soon rebelled against the Medes. In 550 B.C., he was successful in capturing his grandfather Astyages, the Median king, when much of the Median army defected to the side of Cyrus. At this point, the Persian Empire became a "co-empire." Cyrus did not subject the Medes to an annual tribute, and actually made use of their experience as soldiers and administrators in the creation and governing of his empire. The Persian Empire began as the empire of the Medes and Persians, and the Greeks continued to refer to them simply as "the Medes" for several centuries.

With the defeat of Astyages by Cyrus and the fall of the Medes, Nabonidus took advantage of the situation to annex some of the territory conquered and held by the Medes from the Assyrians. The city of Harran and other lands north of Babylon were taken. Harran was the city associated with the god Sin, who

Nabonidus and his mother worshipped. Nabonidus had always wanted to control this land and rebuild the temple to the god Sin in Harran.

The Median/Persian Empire continued to grow, which caused concern among its neighbors, including the nations of Egypt, Babylonia, Sparta and Lydia who joined together in an attempt to stop its expansion. The rich nation of Lydia was the first to fall. The Lydians fought the Persians to a draw, but when they withdrew at the end of the normal campaigning season, they were unexpectedly followed by the Persians who continued the war past the accustomed times. Cyrus captured its capital city and made Lydia a part of the growing Persian Empire.

The Babylonians became Cyrus's next target. He used the dissatisfaction with the rule of Nabonidus as a way of building support for himself inside of Babylon itself. Cyrus presented himself as the leader who the god Marduk had appointed to restore Babylon's true religion to its prominence.

Cyrus' preparations proved successful, and in 539-8 B.C. the Babylonian Empire fell to Cyrus, again helped by defections. The city of Babylon itself, probably the most fortified city in the world, fell to the Persians in a single night and without a fight. Many Babylonians looked at Cyrus as more of a liberator than a conqueror. This theory is supported by the care Cyrus took to maintain a normal way of life in the captured city.

Cyrus extended his rule to the east, then all the way to the Mediterranean in the west. He was very tolerant of the local religious beliefs, which became the norm in his growing empire. He restored the Jews to their lands and allowed them to begin the reconstruction of their temple. He returned the religious artifacts and icons, which had been taken by the Babylonians, to their rightful places.

Cyrus died leading a campaign to the east, and was replaced by his son Cambyses II who was not a friend to the Jews. Work on the temple all but ceased during his rule. Cambyses extended the empire to Egypt. When Cambyses II died, a priest, pretending to be his brother attempted to seize control. Darius, a relative of Cambyses, returned from Egypt, defeated the pretender, and was subsequently made king. Darius was also a benevolent ruler, allowing the Jews and others to continue their religious activities.

Darius' rule was followed by that of Xerxes I, who is probably the Ahasuerus mentioned in Esther. It is also very likely that he is the fourth king mentioned by Daniel (11:2). Xerxes' rule began with revolts in Egypt and Babylon, which were quelled. This prepared his army for an invasion of Greece. As also outlined in Daniel 11:2, Xerxes used the wealth of Persia to assemble a massive army and navy. Daniel foretold that he would "stir up all" against Greece, and Herodotus states that Xerxes assembled his forces from more than forty different nations.

Xerxes was followed by Artaxerxes I, Darius II, Artaxerxes II and III, and Darius III. In about 331 B.C., Alexander the Great conquered Babylon, and the Persian Empire ended. During much of the Persian Empire, there were conflicts with the Greeks. In fact, part of Greece was controlled by the Persians at one time, causing a great deal of resentment there.

Alexander the Great was the son of Philip of Macedonia. Philip, and then his son Alexander, both had the dream of extending Greek culture throughout the world. Philip was successful in conquering and controlling most of Greece, and then Alexander use this base that his father had created and expanded his kingdom into the greatest empire the world had ever seen. He conquered Egypt and Persia, then advanced all the way to the borders of India. As he went, he planted the seeds of Greek culture throughout his empire. He is probably the king spoken of in Daniel 11:3, 4.

Alexander soon died (323), and his empire was

divided up among his generals and administrators, known as the Diadochi. The three main successor groups were the descendants of Ptolemy (Egypt), Seleucus (Middle East), and Antigonus (Macedonia and Asia Minor). These rulers and their successors soon began fighting each other for control of different parts of the former Empire.

The Ptolemy and Seleucid families both claimed the land of Palestine, and fought often for control of the region. In our discussion of Daniel, the Ptolemies are referred to as the kings of the south while the Seleucids are known as the kings of the north. This is the case, at least, through much of Daniel's writings. Several have speculated, also, that some of the references in Daniel are directed at "the end times" instead of the Ptolemaic and Seleucid empires, and that these kings of the north and south are yet unknown.

The Ptolemaic Dynasty began with Ptolemy, who claimed the powers of Pharaoh. The succession of the Ptolemy family was:

> Ptolemy I (Soter I) – 305-282 B.C. – He was one of Alexander's most trusted Generals, and took control of Egypt after Alexander's death. He assumed the traditional role of king, and moved the capital city to Alexandria. He there established a center for culture and learning, and proved to be a practical and effective leader.

> Ptolemy II (Philadelphus) – 282-246 B.C. – He assumed co-regency with his father in 284 B.C. and became sole ruler after his father's death. He directed the construction of a canal leading from the Nile River to the Gulf of Suez. He also continued is

father's passion for learning, and was credited for the gathering of seventy-two Jewish scholars who were said to have translated the Hebrew Scriptures to Greek, eventually creating the Septuagint (LXX).

Ptolemy III (Euergetes I) – 246-222 B.C. – He continued a tradition started by his father, and married his full sister Berenice. There was conflict with the Seleucids during his reign.

Ptolemy IV (Philopator I) – 222-205 B.C. – He also married his sister, Arsinoe, and established a cult worshipping them as the Father-loving Gods. After his death, his wife was murdered.

Ptolemy V (Epiphanes) – 205-180 B.C. – Egypt was weakened early in his rule when the kingdoms from Macedonia and Syria joined to take Egypt's foreign possessions. The Rosetta Stone, which unlocked the understanding of the Egyptian language, was written during his reign. He married the Seleucid princess Cleopatra I.

Ptolemy VI (Philometer) – 180-145 B.C. – He was defeated by the Seleucid king Antiochus IV (Epiphanes). Ptolemy VIII, his brother, was given the throne. Later the two ruled as co-regents, and eventually split the kingdom with Ptolemy VI ruling Egypt and Ptolemy VIII ruling the western province of Cyrenaica.

Ptolemy VII (Neos Philopator) – 145 B.C. - He was a boy when assuming the throne, and was soon murdered by Ptolemy VIII.

Ptolemy VIII (Euergetes II) – 145-116 B.C. – From 163 to 145 he was King in Cyrenaica, Libya. He assumed the throne by killing his nephew at the wedding feast where he married the boy's mother. He was responsible for dividing Egypt from Cyrenaica. He also married his wife's daughter Cleopatra III, who he designated his successor.

This begins a period of frequent changes in rule. Cleopatra III ruled with her sons for several years, and her rule lasted until 80 B.C. There followed frequent struggles between competing claimants, and this lasted until Cleopatra VII and Ptolemy XIII (52-30 B.C.). This is the Cleopatra of Caesar and Mark Antony fame, who was the final ruler in the Ptolemy line.

The Seleucids dynasty began with Seleucus I (Nicator) who was, like Ptolemy I, a general under Alexander the Great. The succession of Seleucid rulers was:

Seleucus I (Nicator) – 312-280 B.C. - Founder of the Seleucid Dynasty.

He was originally the Satrap of Babylon, but made himself king soon after Alexander's death. Helped defeat Antigonus I of Macedonia, and took control of Syria and much of Asia Minor. He was responsible for the construction of several cities, including Antioch.

Antiochus I (Soter) - 280-261 B.C. – Son of Seleucus I, he was successful against the Galatians, but lost a great deal of land to Ptolemy II.

Antiochus II (Theos) - 261-247 B.C. – He waged a long, costly war and was able to regain much of the land his father had lost to Ptolemy II. Internal divisions, however, cost him the provinces of Bactria and Parthia.

Seleucus II (Callinicus) - 247-226 B.C. – Was involved in the Third Syrian War with Ptolemy III, and was unable to stop the Egyptians from invading Syria and Mesopotamia. He also lost land in other areas.

Seleucus III (Ceraunus) – 226-223 B.C. – Attempted to consolidate what was left of the empire's strength; he went to war in Asia Minor where he was assassinated.

Antiochus III (The Great) - 223-187 B.C. - Brother to Seleucus III, he was one of the most successful of the

Seleucid line. He conquered Parthia and Bactria, and waged a successful campaign against Ptolemy V in which he took control of Palestine. He was eventually defeated by the Romans, and lost control of the lands on the eastern Mediterranean.

Seleucus IV (Philopator) – 187-175 B.C. – Ruled over a period of recovery from the empire's defeats. He was forced to place heavy taxes on the people in order to pay the Romans. He was assassinated by one of his ministers.

Antiochus IV (Epiphanes) - 175-164 B.C. – The son of Antiochus III, he was the ruler most associated with the prophecies of Daniel. He fought several successful wars against Ptolemies VI and VIII, and was able to divide Egypt into two parts. After being forced by the Romans to withdraw from Egypt, he returned and captured Jerusalem. He attempted to destroy the Jewish religion and was able to replace the traditional temple worship with sacrifice to Zeus. He was defeated in Judah by forces led by the Maccabees.

Antiochus V (Eupator) – 164-162 B.C. – The nine-year-old son of Antiochus IV, his rule was controlled by his regent, Lysias.

Demetrius I (Soter) – 162-150 B.C. – He was the son of Seleucus IV, and escaped from Rome where he was being kept hostage. He returned and proclaimed himself king. Lysias was unable to maintain power, and he and Antiochus V were murdered. Demetrius was killed fighting against the Egyptians.

In the general history of the region, in conjunction with the Ptolemies, there occurred a succession of rulers. Jerusalem was recaptured, but the empire continued to erode. Constant infighting weakened the empire to the point where Rome moved in and assumes control unopposed.

The history of the Jews, located in Egypt, Babylon and Palestine, was largely a history of the dynamics between two dynasties, the Seleucid and the Ptolemy. The Jews in Palestine found themselves in frequent peril from one invading army or the other.

In way of review and amplification of the history, we know that these two kingdoms were among those created after the death of Alexander the Great and the division of his empire. This period was called the Diadochi Wars, and was a period of shifting interests and allegiances. At times, Seleucus and Ptolemy were allies, and at other times they were enemies. In 301 B.C., Ptolemy took control of Palestine and became the enemy of Seleucus. Then later, in 288, they were allies against Demetrius.

The next generation of rulers enjoyed a similar relationship. About 274 B.C. Ptolemy II began the First Syrian War by advancing into Asia Minor and gaining control of the Syrian coast. After year of conflict and mistrust, Ptolemy II and Antiochus II made peace. At this time, Ptolemy II gave his daughter, Berenice, to Antiochus and they were married as a confirmation of this alliance. Soon after the marriage Ptolemy died, and Antiochus took back Laodice, the wife he had put aside for Berenice.

Laodice apparently wanted revenge. Antiochus, Berenice, the child of their marriage, and Berenice's attendants were all soon dead. This situation was avenged by Berenice's brother, Ptolemy III who then ruled in Egypt. Ptolemy III advanced into Syria, had Laodice put to death and moved through the land as far east as the Tigris River.

Besides avenging the death of his sister, Ptolemy seized much of the wealth of the land, including many of the religious artifacts from the different temples. This included many of those taken from Egypt by Cambyses, when he conquered that land.

Seleucus II had moved his armies away to the east during this time, and after Ptolemy returned to Egypt, he moved back toward Syria and regained control of much of the land which had been lost. The land of Palestine, however, remained under control of the Egyptians. About 240 B.C. Seleucus II attempted to attack Egypt, but without success.

Seleucus son, Antiochus III was finally successful in reclaiming more of the lost lands from the Egyptians. He not only recaptured the entire Syrian kingdom, which was occupied by Egypt, but eventually managed to extend his control to Palestine.

Antiochus the Great achieved his success against Ptolemy IV, who was somewhat indolent, preferring the comforts of his court to battle. These defeats, however, finally angered Ptolemy who raised a significant force and defeated the Syrian army in Palestine, inflicting heavy losses on the Syrians. Ptolemy did not follow up on his victory, and simply returned to his life of luxury. Antiochus, in the meantime, turned his attentions to the eastern part of his kingdom.

When the teenage Ptolemy V ascended to the throne, Antiochus the Great and Philip of Macedonia combined to take advantage of the inexperienced young monarch and conquer some of Egypt's foreign holdings. Antiochus was able to retake Palestine in 203 B.C. but the Egyptians soon pushed them back once more. Later, the Seleucids returned to Palestine and were able to establish permanent control over the Jewish people.

Peace eventually returned, and the two great nations sealed this new situation with another marriage. Antiochus formalized this arrangement by having his daughter, Cleopatra, marry young Ptolemy. If Antiochus' goal was to introduce an advocate for Seleucid interests in the Egyptian courts, this did not happen. Cleopatra instead integrated herself into Egyptian life and soon became a part of the ongoing drama of the Ptolemies.

Supposedly having secured his southern border, Antiochus attempted to expand northward. Besides part of Asia Minor, Antiochus was able to establish a foothold in Greece. By this time, he had received the aid of Hannibal of Carthage, and was beginning to move deeper into Greece. The Romans sent the general Scipio Asiaticus to stop him, which ultimately resulted in Antiochus being forced to return not only the land taken in Greece, but relinquish much of the land in Asia Minor which he controlled.

Antiochus the Great was followed by his

son Seleucus IV. Seleucus found himself under obligation to pay a heavy tribute to the Romans, and was left with an empty treasury with which to do it. He was therefore forced to impose a heavier tax burden on the nation, and finally to send collectors out to take the wealth of many of the religious shrines and other cities he controlled.

Seleucus died, probably assassinated, after a few years. The next ruler of the Seleucid Empire was Antiochus IV, Epiphanes, who occupies much of the prophecy found in Daniel 11. Antiochus IV was not the rightful heir. Demetrius I was the son of Seleucus, but was being held hostage in Rome. Antiochus Epiphanes hurried back and promptly seized the throne by conspiring with people inside and outside of Syria.

Antiochus fought several wars with Egypt. When he became strong enough, Antiochus took back Palestine, which had been given to the Egyptians with the marriage of Cleopatra to Ptolemy. Antiochus attempted to manipulate the rulers in Egypt, but was unsuccessful.

Another important element which characterized the rule of Antiochus, was his effort to stamp out the Jewish religion. He replaced Onias, the rightful Zadokite High Priest, with his brother Jason. Jason was given the High Priesthood because of a substantial bribe to Epiphanes and a promise to initiate a program of Hellenization among the Jews.

In 172 B.C., Menelaus made Antiochus a better offer, and was made High Priest. Menelaus returned to Jerusalem and pillaged the temple to pay the bribe. A few years later, when Antiochus was forced to put down a rebellion in Palestine, Menelaus allowed the king to enter the Temple and remove several sacred items.

In 168 B.C., when Antiochus Epiphanes was prevented from invading Egypt by the Romans, he took out his anger on the hated Jews. Since he had with him a substantial army, the Jews were unable to prevent him from doing has he wished, which was to prohibit any of the traditional Jewish ceremonies and the reading of the Torah; all of this done with the support of Menelaus.

The most egregious act was the desecration of the Temple, sometimes called the fortress or sanctuary. Antiochus ended all of the traditional ceremonies, and substituted a sacrifice to the Greek god Zeus.

This replacement of the traditional sacrifice for a sacrifice to Zeus/Jupiter, begun in the temple at Jerusalem, then spread throughout the country. In the town of Modin, however, a priest named Mattathias killed the Jewish priest who agreed to conduct this sacrifice, along with the king's representative sent to oversee it. This was the beginning of the Maccabean revolt.

The revolt was soon joined by the Hasidim, or pious ones. The revolt continued to grow and eventually, along with Roman support, it forced Antiochus to rescind his hated reforms. These changes came too late, and the Maccabees succeeded in retaking and purifying the temple three years after its desecration.

Antiochus IV died in 164 B.C., and Lysias became regent for the nine-year-old Antiochus V. Lysias was forced to grant religious autonomy to the Jews. The old High Priest Menelaus was killed, and Alcimus was accepted by the Jews as his replacement. The rebellion continued, and after some success, Judas Maccabeus was killed.

The war continued, and Jonathan Maccabeus took advantage of the rivalries among the Seleucid leadership to become both the political and the religious leader of the Jews. It is quite possible that this is the time when a new group, which would eventually establish the community at Qumran, began. Alcimus died in 159 B.C., and there is no record of who replaced him as High Priest.

In 152 B.C, we do know that there was some opposition when the Hasmonean leader, Jonathan, received the High Priesthood. The office of High Priest had traditionally belonged to the Zadokite line (Zadok was High Priest during the times of David and Solomon), and many conservative Jews resisted the appointment of a Hasmonean.

Some speculate that the "Wicked Priest," who was a significant figure in the culture at Qumran was Jonathan. Also, that the High Priest deposed by him, or a similarly important religious leader during this time, was the "Teacher of Righteousness" who was forced to leave Jerusalem. It is suggested by some that the deposed High Priest was in some way instrumental in the formation of this religious community. This would place the establishment of Qumran at about 150 B.C.

Jonathan was eventually captured by the Syrians and executed. His brother Simon replaced him in about 142 B.C. Over the next few decades, the Jews were in regular conflict with the Seleucids. They were able to achieve a brief period of independence under Simon and others.

In 63 B.C., the Romans took Jerusalem and began their rule. The Romans first appointed Antipater, then his son Herod the Great, as kings over much of the land. Herod's rule was somewhat contradictory, as he expanded and refurbished the Temple in Jerusalem, making it one of the most beautiful buildings in the world. At the same time, he attempted to spread Greek culture and learning throughout the land.

After Herod's death, his kingdom was divided into three parts and given to his sons. After the death of Herod the Great's son Herod Agrippa, they Jews were put under direct Roman rule. In 66 A.D., the Roman governor attempted to reinforce this control by repression and murder, which soon led to open revolt among the Jews. Vespasian and his son Titus invaded Palestine, and after a campaign and siege of several years put down the insurgency. During this time, Vespasian became emperor, and the historian Josephus came to support Roman rule. All Jewish resistance was crushed, with places like Masada being isolated and ultimately destroyed.

With the final defeat of the Jews, the city of Jerusalem was completely destroyed. With the temple gone, the Jewish religion became significantly different. The priesthood and sacrificial rites were discontinued, and power passed to the Rabbis. One group of Rabbi, which had supported the Romans in their attack on Jerusalem, set up a school in Jamnia.

A second Jewish revolt took place some sixty years later, and resulted in the Jews being expelled completely from their homeland. The name of the lands and the cities were all changed, and for a time circumcision was forbidden. From this time on, the Jews disappeared as a unified political body. They did, none the less, preserve their religious and cultural identity.

GLOSSARY

Allegory – The method of textual interpretation in which there are levels of meaning. The surface meaning represents some deeper message. It was used by the Jews and Christians in their writings.

Allusion – To refer to something without making a direct reference.

Amanuensis – A scribe who takes down the dictation from the actual 'writer' of the text.

Apocalyptic – A world view which anticipates and end where God's will assert himself directly into the world.

Apocryphal – The designation of books in the Greek Old Testament, usually considered scriptural by the Catholic or Orthodox churches that are not included in the Protestant or Hebrew scriptures.

Aramaic – A Semitic language, from the same family as Hebrew. It was the common spoken language in the near east until Alexander the Great. It was originally divided into two groups, Eastern and Western, but now an Imperial or Official Aramaic has been identified which was the administrative language of the Neo-Babylonian and Persian Empires. Aramaic remained the common language in Palestine until the time of Christ.

Authenticity – When a work is correctly attributed to its actual author.

Autograph – The original copy of a text. Using Daniel as a reference, it is the final copy prepared by the author, which was then released for distribution.

Book of the Twelve – (see Minor Prophets)

Canon – An official list of book accepted as Scripture

Canonisation – The process by which a book is accepted in to canon that is accepted as Scripture.

Chiasm – A literary technique, common in Semitic literature, in which a parallel structure is created, following a pattern like ABC-CBA.

Codex – A book which is read by turning its pages, usually between two text here. covers. Became the common way of writing scriptures during the Christian period.

Conflation – The process by which two different versions of a text grow together and are eventually combined.

Covenant – A special bond between God and His people, which places obligations or promises on both parties.

Critic – For this study, someone who accepts the late date of authorship, and denies that Daniel was actually the author of the book.

Cuneiform – A system of writing used anciently in Mesopotamia and the Near East. The characters are inscribed into clay tablets using a wedge shaped tool.

Dead Sea Scrolls - A collection of texts found in caves near Qumran, by the Dead Sea. They belonged to a Jewish sect from around the time of Christ.

Deuterocanonical – The Roman Catholic name for the

Apocrypha.

Deuteronimistic History – Scholarly name for Joshua, Judges, Samuel and Kings because of their dependence on the ideas of Deuteronomy.

Early date – The theory for the dating of the book of Daniel that places it in the sixth century B.C. This implies the author was Daniel for whom the book was named.

Epistle – Ancient name for a letter.

Eschatology – Religious teachings regarding the last days or end of times.

Exile – The removal of the Jews from Judah, caused by their rebellion and resulting in the destruction of Jerusalem and the Temple. This occurred in 598 and 587 B.C.

Gnosticism – Teaching presented as being based on a 'special knowledge' in the early Christian era.

Israel – Initially it represented the covenant people of God, but later became the name of the northern kingdom with its capital in Samaria

Johannine – Teaching based on the writings of the Apostle John.

Judah – Southern of the two Hebrew kingdoms, with its capital in Jerusalem.

Hagiographa – This is the section of the Hebrew Scriptures know as the writings.

Hexapala – The work of the early Christian Origen, who listed six versions of the Old Testament side by side.

Kaige – A Greek recension of the Old Testament from about the first century B.C. Some believe it to be the basis for Theodotion's version.

Late date – The theory for the dating of the book of Daniel

that places it in the second century B.C. This implies the book is pseudepigraphal, and not the work of Daniel himself.

Lucianic Recension – A Greek revision of the Old Testament prepared by the Christian Martyr Lucian. It also was prepared to more closely reflect the Hebrew Scriptures.

LXX – (see Septuagint)

Maccabees – Jewish rebels who successful fought Antiochus Epiphanes. They rebelled when the repression of the Jewish rebellion became too oppressive.

Masoretes – (see Masoretic)

Masoretic (Massoretic) – Referring to texts produced by Jewish scholars (called Masoretes) who assumed the task of faithfully transmitting the Bible. These scholars also added vowels and punctuation to the text, vowel points (the original of the Hebrew text contains only consonants).

Minor Prophets – In the Christian Old Testament they are: Hosea, Joel, Amos, Obadiah, Jonah, Micah, Nahum, Habakkuk, Zephaniah, Haggai, Zechariah, and Malachi. They are called Minor Prophets based mainly in the size of the book as opposed to importance.

Mishnah – The Jewish collection of rulings regarding the Torah, collected about the second century A.D.

Old Greek – A collection of Greek translations of Old Testament books. Some believe it formed the basis for the Septuagint version.

Papyrus – A reed grown in Egypt used in the preparation of paper, also referred to as papyrus. It was a major writing material in Biblical times.

Pastoral Epistles – Paul's letters relating to the ministry to the saints. These were written to Timothy and Titus.

Patristic – Related to the writing of the early Christian 'Fathers' of the first century A.D.

Pauline – Ideas and teachings based on the writings of the Apostle Paul.

Pentateuch – The first five books of the Bible, the books of Moses.

Pseudonymous – A work written by someone using the name of another famous, usually historical, person.

Q – A hypothetical book proposed by many as the original source for much of the information in the Gospels.

Rabbinical – Attributed to the Rabbis, or Jewish teachers. They were formed from the Pharisees and were responsible for the standardization of Jewish practice and scripture.

Recension – A textual revision created by combining the best information regarding the text from available sources.

Scribe – A profession based on the ability to write, not exclusively in the area of religion.

Septuagint – The Greek translation of the Bible popular at the time of Christ. It was said to be the work of seventy scribes in Alexandria, Egypt. It was translated from one of the traditions of the Hebrew scriptures between the third and first centuries B.C.

Synoptic Gospels – The gospels of Matthew, Mark and Luke which present a similar story of Christ.

Talmud – The collection of rabbinic commentary on the Mishnah.

Theodotion – A Greek version of the Old Testament which followed the LXX version. It was prepared by Theodotus from whom the name was taken. It was prepared to more closely follow the Hebrew scripture.

Torah – The instructions by which Jewish life is to be conducted, similar to the law. It is sometimes used synonymously with Pentateuch.

Vorlage – The textual version of a book before it was translated.

BIBLIOGRAPHY

Press Release, April 11, 1995. University of Arizona Department of Physics. Tuscon, AZ.

Eusebius. 325 AD. *Ecclesiastical History.*

Africa, Thomas W. 1969. *The Ancient World.* Boston: Houghton Mifflin Company.

Allen, Clilfton J. (General Editor). 1971. *The Broadman Bible Commentary, Vol.6.* Nashville, TN: Broadman Press.

Baldwin, Joyce G. 1978. *Daniel, An Introduction and Commentary.* Madison, WI: Inter-Varsity Press.

Brownlee, William Hugh. 1964. *The Meaning of the Qumran Scrolls for the Bible, Special Attention to Isaiah.* New York: Oxford University Press.

Davies, Philip R. 1993. *Daniel.* Sheffield, England: Journal for the Study of the Old Testament.

Driver, S.R. 1898. *An Introduction to the Literature of the Old Testament Eighth Edition).* New York: Charles Scribner's Sons.

Dummelow, J. R. (Editor). 1974. *A Commentary on the Holy Bible.* New York: McMillan Publishing Co., Inc.

Eiselen, Frederick Carl (Editor). 1929. *The Abingdon Bible Commentary.* New York: Abingdon-Cokesbury Press.

Eusebius. *Praeparatio Evangelica.*

Fohrer, Georg. 1968. *Introduction to the Old Testament*. Nashville, TN: Abingdon Press.

Frank, Harry Thomas. 1971. *Bible, Archaeology, and Faith*. Nashville, TN: Abingdon Press.

Gordon, Cyrus H. 1965. *The Ancient Near East, 3rd Edition*. New York: WW Norton & Co.

1958. *The World of the Old Testament*. Garden City, NJ: Doubleday.

Gowan, Donald E. 2001. "Daniel" *Abingdon Old Testament Commentaries*. Nashville, TN: Abingdon Press.

Harrison, Roland Kenneth. 1969. *Introduction to the Old Testament*. Grand Rapids, MI: Eerdmans Publishing Co.

Hartman, Louis Francis. 1978. *The Book of Daniel (Anchor Bible, Vol. 23)*. Garden City, NY: Doubleday & Company, Inc.

Herodotus. 450 A.D. *The History of Herodotus*.

Josephus, Flavius. *Antiquities of the Jews*.

Kuhl, Curt (translated C.T.M. Herriott). 1962. *The Old Testament, Its Origins and Composition*. Richmond VA: John Knox Press.

Larue, Gerald A. 1975. *Ancient Myth and Modern Man*. Englewood Cliffs, N.J.: Prentice-Hall, Inc.

Laymon, Charles M. (Editor). 1983. *Interpreters Concise Commentary: Vol. IV: The Major Prophets*. Nashville, TN: Abingdon Press.

Laymon, Charles M. (Editor). 1971. *Interpreter's One-Volume Commentary on the Bible*. Nashville, TN: Abingdon Press.

Mansoor, Menahem. 1965. The Dead Sea Scrolls: *A College Textbook and a Study Guide*. Grand Rapids, MI: Wm. B. Eerdmans.

Meadowcroft, T.J. 1995. *Aramaic Daniel and Greek Daniel, A Literary Comparison*. Scheffield, England: Journal for the Study of the Old Testament.

Michael Wise, Robert W. 1994. *The Dead Sea Scrolls Uncovered*. New York: Barnes and Noble Books.

Motyer, J. A., and D. Guthrie. 1991. *New Bible Commentary*. Grand Rapids, MI: Eerdmans Publishing Co.

O'Flaherty, Wendy Doniger. 1979. *The Critical Study of Sacred Texts*. Berkeley, CA: Berkely Religious Studies Series.

Pfeiffer, Robert H. 1953. *Introduction to the Old Testament*. London: A & C Black, Ltd.

Pritchard, James B. 1958. *Archaeology and the Old Testament*. Princeton, NJ: Princeton University Press.

Pritchard, James B. 1973. *The Ancient Near East, Vol 1, an Anthology of Text and Pictures*. Princeton, N.J.: Princeton University Press.

Pritchard, James B. 1975. *The Ancient Near East, Vol 2, A New Anthology of Texts and Pictures*. Princeton, N.J.: Princeton University Press.

Rendsburg, Gary A., and Cyrus H. Gordon. 1997. *The Bible and the Ancient Near East*. New York: W. W. Norton and Co.

Rennie, Bryan. 2002. Religion 101: Understanding the Bible: Daniel. In *Westminster University Staff: Dr. Bryan S. Rennie* [Online]. Wilmington, PA: Westminster University, 2002 [cited 23 May, 2002]. Currently available on World Wide Web: <http://www.westminster.edu/staff/brennie/daniel.htm>.

Rogerson, John (Editor). 2001. *The Oxford Illustrated History of the Bible*. Oxford, England: Oxford University Press.

Ross, Sir E. Denison. 1931. *The Persians*. Oxford, England: The Oxford University Pres.

Roux, George. 1992. *Ancient Iraq, Third Edition*. London, England: Penguin Books.

Saggs, H. W. F. 1989. *Civilization Before Greece and Rome*. New Haven, CT: Yale University Press.

Schiffman, Lawrence H. 1995. *Reclaiming the Dead Sea Scrolls*. New York: The Anchor Bible Reference.

Shanks, Hershel. 1992. *The Dead Sea Scrolls After Forty Years*. Washington, D.C: Biblical Archaeology Society.

Shaw, Ian (Editor). 2000. *The Oxford History of Ancient Egypt*. Oxford, UK: Oxford University Press.

Shea, William H. 1991. Darius the Mede in His Persian-Babylonian Setting, In *Andrews Univ. Seminary Studies 1991*. Berrien Springs: Andrews University Press.

Soggin, J. Alberto. 1976. *Introduction to the Old Testament*. Philadelphia: The Westminster Press.

Strong, James. 1990. *Strong's Exhaustive Concordance of the Bible*. Nashville, TN: Thomas Nelson Publishers.

Till, Farrell. 2001. Bad History in the Book of Daniel, In *The Skeptic Review* [Online]. *http://www.infidels.org/library/magazines/tsr/index.shtml*.

von Soden, Wolfram. 1994. *The Ancient Orient*. Grand Rapids, MI: Eerdmans Publishing Company.

Walton, John H. and Andrew E. Hill. 1991. *A Survey of the Old Testament*. Grand Rapids, MI: Zondervan Publishing House.

Wood, Leon J. 1990. *A Commentary on Daniel*. Grand Rapids, MI: Regency Reference Library.

Wright, G. Ernest. 1957. *Biblical Archaeology*. Philadelphia : The Westminster Press.

Yamauchi, Edwin M. 2000. Persia and the Bible. Grand Rapids, MI: Baker Books.

Young, Edward J. 1949. An Introduction to the Old Testament. Grand Rapids, MI: Wm. B. Eerdmans Publishing Co.

Young, Edward, and Wilson, Robert. 1959. *A Scientific Investigation of the Old Testament*. Chicago, Il: Moody Press.

ENDNOTES

[1] Louis Francis Hartman, *The Book of Daniel (Anchor Bible, Vol. 23)* (Garden City, NY: Doubleday & Company, 1978), p. 9.

[2] Cyrus H. Gordon and Gary Rendsburg, *The Bible and the Ancient Near East* (New York: W.W. Norton and Company, 1997), p. 79.

[3] Robert H. Pfeiffer, *Introduction to the Old Testament* (London, England: A & C Black, Ltd, 1953), p. 761.

[4] Joyce G. Baldwin, *Daniel, An Introduction and Commentary* (Madison, WI: Inter-Varsity Press, 1978), p. 40.

[5] Robert H. Pfieffer, "Daniel" in *Introduction to the Old Testament* (London: A&C Black, Ltd, 1953), p.756.

[6] Cyrus H. Gordon and Gary A. Rendsburg, *The Bible and the Ancient Near East* (New York: W. W. Norton and Co., 1997), p. 312.

[7] Frederick Carl Eiselen, ed., "Daniel" in *The Abingdon Bible Commentary* (New York: Abingdon-Cokesbury Press, 1929), p. 747.

[8] Georg Fohrer, *Introduction to the Old Testament* (Nashville: Abingdon, 1968), p. 472.

[9] *Ibid.*, p. 477

[10] Pfieffer, "Daniel", p. 765.

[11] Eiselen, *The Abingdon Bible Commentary*, p. 748.

[12] Philip R. Davies, "Daniel" *Journal for the Study of the Old Testament* (Sheffield, England: Scheffield Academic Press, 1993), p. 30.
[13] Wolfram von Soden, *The Ancient Orient* (Grand Rapids: Eerdman's Publishing, 1994), p. 48.
[14] Baldwin, *Daniel*, p.20.
[15] Ian Shaw, ed., *The Oxford History of Ancient Egypt* (Oxford, UK: Oxford University Press, 2000), p. 381.
[16] Farrell Till, "Bad History in the Book of Daniel" from *The Skeptic's Review* (online: www.infidels.org/library/magazines/tsr/1998/984bad.html, 1998).
[17] S.R. Driver, *An Introduction to the Literature of the Old Testament*, Eighth Edition (New York: Charles Scribner's Sons, 1898), p. 498.
[18] Eiselen, *The Abingdon Bible Commentary*, p. 749
[19] Bryan Rennie, "The Dating of the Book of Daniel" from course material of Religion 101:Understanding the Bible, Westminster University.
[20] von Soden, *The Ancient Orient*, p. 60.
[21] J.R. Dummelow, ed., *A Commentary on the Holy Bible* (New York: McMillan Publishing Co., Inc, 1974), p. 530.
[22] James Strong, *Strong's Exhaustive Concordance of the Bible* (Nashville, TN: Thomas Nelson Publishers, 1990), pp. 737, 738.
[23] Pfeiffer, *Introduction*, p. 756.
[24] Baldwin, *Daniel*, p. 29.
[25] Philip R. Davies, *Daniel*, p. 38.
[26] Driver, *An Introduction*, p. 498.
[27] Donald E. Gowan, *Daniel* (Nashville, TN: Abingdon Press, 2001), p. 57.
[28] Pfeiffer, *Introduction*, p. 757
[29] Gowan, *Daniel*, p. 58.
[30] Eusebius, *Praeparatio Evangelica*, IX.
[31] Dr. Leon J. Wood, *A Commentary on Daniel* (Grand Rapids, MI: Zondervan Publishing House, 1990), p. 121.

[32] Till, "Bad History."
[33] Edwin Yamauchi, *Persia and the Bible* (Grand Rapids, MI: Baker Books, 2000), p. 51.
[34] James B. Pritchard, ed. *The Ancient Near East, Vol 2, A New Anthology of Texts and Pictures* (Princeton, NJ: Princeton University Press, 1975), p. 107.
[35] Georges Roux, *Ancient Iraq (Third Edition)* (London, England: Penguin Books, 1992), p. 381.
[36] Driver, *Introduction,* p. 498.
[37] David Hughes, *Egypt2Britain: Queen Hatshepsut to H.M. Queen Elizabeth*, 2002. Personal correspondence confirms that this portion of the genealogical table was constructed from and is confirmed by: Ronald H. Sack, *Amel-Marduk: 562-560 B.C.* (1972); G.R. Tabouis, *Nebuchadnezzar.* (1977); Donald J. Wiseman (ed.), *Chronicles of Chaldean Kings,* (1956); and the *Journal of Ancient and Medireview Studies,* vol. XII, page 55.
[38] Driver, *Introduction,* p. 499.
[39] Ibid, p. 498.
[40] Roux, *Ancient Iraq,* p. 386.
[41] *Ibid,* p. 339.
[42] Davies, *Daniel,* p. 30.
[43] James B. Pritchard, ed., *The Ancient Near East, Vol.1, an Anthology of Text and Pictures* (Princeton, NJ: Princeton University Press, 1973), p. 204.
[44] Thomas W. Africa, *The Ancient World* (Boston: Houghton Mifflin Company, 1969), p. 49.
[45] Yamauchi, p.
[46] Sir E. Denison Ross, *ThePersians* (Oxford, England: Oxford University Press, 1931), p. 33.
[47] *Ibid.*
[48] Pritchard, *Ancient Near East, Vol.1,* p. 204.
[49] Driver, *Introduction,* p. 500.
[50] Till, "Bad History;" Pfieffer, "Daniel," p. 757.
[51] William H. Shea, "Darius the Mede in His Persian-Babylonian Setting," *Andrews University Seminary Studies, Vol. 29, No.3* (Autumn 1991): 252-253.

[52] Charles M. Laymon, ed., "Daniel," *Interpreter's One-Volume Commentary on the Bible* (Nashville, TN: Abingdon Press, 1971), p. 447.
[53] Pritchard, *Ancient Near East, Vol.* 1, p. 204.
[54] Pritchard, *Ancient Near East*, Vol. 1, p. 204.
[55] Cites Shae, "Unrecognized Vassal King," *Andrews University Seminary Studies* (9: 1971), p. 113.
[56] Yamauchi, Persia, p. 89.
[57] Africa, *Ancient World*, p. 49.
[58] Pfieffer, "Daniel," p. 757
[59] Yamauchi, *Persian*, p. 38.
[60] G. Ernest Wright, *Biblical Archaeology* (Philadelphia: The Westminster Press, 1957), p. 161.
[61] Baldwin, *Daniel*, p. 27.
[62] Shea, "Persian-Babylonian Setting," pp. 235-257.
[63] Pfieffer, *Introduction*, p. 754.
[64] Wood, *Commentary*, p. 16.
[65] Driver, *Introduction*, p. 498.
[66] Charles M. Laymon, ed, Interpreters Concise Commentary: Vol. IV: The Major Prophets (Nashville, TN: Abingdon Press, 1983), p. 309.
[67] Laymon, "Daniel," p. 436.
[68] Driver, *Introduction*, p. 509.
[69] William H. Brownlee, *The Meaning of the Qumran Scrolls for the Bible, Special Attention to Isaiah* (Oxford, England: Oxford University Press, 1964), p. 48.
[70] Louis Francis Hartman, *The Book of Daniel (Anchor Bible, Vol. 23)* (Garden City, New York: Doubleday & Co., 1978), p. 25.
[71] Lawrence H. Schiffman, *Reclaiming the Dead Sea Scrolls* (New York: Doubleday Books, 1995), p. 162.
[72] Hartman, *Daniel,* p. 43.
[73] *Ibid.,* p. 77.
[74] T. J. Meadowcroft, *Aramaic Daniel and Greek Daniel, A Literary Comparison* (Scheffield, England: Scheffield Academic Press, 1995), p. 25.

[75] Menahem Mansoor, The Dead Sea Scrolls: A College Textbook and a Study Guide (Wm B Eerdmans: Grand Rapids, MI, 1965), p. 82.
[76] Wendy Doniger O'Flaherty,ed., *The Critical Study of Sacred Texts* (Berkeley, CA: Berkeley Religious Studies Series, 1979), p. 44.
[77] Meadocroft, *Aramaic Daniel*, p. 262.
[78] Hartman, *Daniel*, p. 78.
[79] John Rogerson, ed., *The Oxford Illustrated History of the Bible* (Oxford, England: Oxford University Press, 2001); p. 72.
[80] Meadowcroft, *Aramaic Daniel*, p. 15.
[81] O'Flaherty, *Critical Study*, p. 47.
[82] Ibid., p. 48.
[83] Driver, *Literature*, p. 508.
[84] Pfeiffer, *Introduction*, p. 757.
[85] Driver, *Literature*, p. 502.
[86] Eiselen, *Abingdon*, p. 747.
[87] Davies, *Daniel*, p. 37.
[88] Hartman, *Daniel*, p. 74.
[89] H.W.F. Saggs, *Civilization Before Greece and Rome* (New Haven, CT: Yale University Press, 1989), p. 32. (Cites D.L. Wiseman, *Notes on some Problems in the Book of Daniel*, London: Tyndale, 1965, p. 75)
[90] Baldwin, *Daniel*, p. 31
[91] Cyrus H. Gordon, *The Ancient Near East, 3rd Edition* (New York: W.W. Norton, 1965), p. 20.
[92] Davies, *Daniel*, p. 38.
[93] Yamauchi, *Persia*, p. 380.
[94] Harry Thomas Frank, *Bible, Archaeology, and Faith* (Nashville, TN: Abingdon Press, 1971), p. 222.
[95] Yamauchi, *Persia*, 98,
[96] Alfred Sendry, *Music in Ancient Israel* (New York: Philosophical Library, 1969), p. 297.
[97] Baldwin, *Daniel*, p. 33.
[98] Baldwin, *Daniel*, p. 33. (Cites K. A. Kitchen, *Notes on Some Problems in the Book of Daniel*, London: Tyndale, p. 35-44)

[99] Meadowcroft, *Aramaic Daniel*, p. 277.
[100] Shiffman, *Reclaiming,* p. 123.
[101] Robert W. Eisenman and Michael Wise, *The Dead Sea Scrolls Uncovered* (New York: Barnes and Noble Books, 1994), p. 137.
[102] Ibid., p. 41.
[103] Brownlee, *Meaning,* p. 30.
[104] O'Flaherty, *Critical Study,* p. 49.
[105] Hartman, *Daniel*, p. 77.

www.ingramcontent.com/pod-product-compliance
Lightning Source LLC
Chambersburg PA
CBHW060824050426
42453CB00008B/577